LETTERS
from a
Distinguished
American

LETTERS
from a
DISTINGUISHED
AMERICAN

*Twelve Essays by John Adams
on American Foreign Policy, 1780*

Compiled and Edited by JAMES H. HUTSON

Coordinator, American Revolution Bicentennial Program

LIBRARY OF CONGRESS   WASHINGTON   1978

Frontispiece: *John Adams. After a John Singleton Copley painting, 1783. From Worthington Chauncey Ford*, George Washington *(New York: Charles Schribner's Sons; and Paris: Goupil & Co., 1900).*

LIBRARY OF CONGRESS CATALOGING IN PUBLICATION DATA

Adams, John, Pres. U. S., 1735–1826.
  Letters from a distinguished American.

  Includes bibliographical references.
  1. United States History—Revolution, 1775–1783—Sources. 2. Adams, John, Pres. U. S., 1735–1826. 3. Galloway, Joseph, 1731–1803. I. Hutson, James H. II. Title.
E203.A57   973.3'2   77-25356
ISBN 0–8444–0258–3

For sale by the Superintendent of Documents, U.S. Government Printing Office
Washington, D.C. 20402

Stock No. 030–000–00095–1

Preface

THE LETTERS published in this volume were discovered in the course of sampling the Library of Congress's collections of foreign newspapers published during the American Revolution to ascertain the value and the feasibility of a project to enlist the cooperation of librarians and archivists in several nations to bring these newspapers under bibliographic control and to make them more accessible to students of the Revolution. The importance of Adams's letters—virtually unknown and never reprinted—is a testimony to the untapped riches which exist in the foreign newspapers of the period. It is hoped that their publication will inspire efforts to collect and exploit these newspapers in a systematic manner.

I have supplied an essay describing the context in which Adams wrote his letters and exploring the conduit through whom they reached publication, the enigmatic Edmund Jenings. An appendix is devoted to an unknown chapter in the diplomacy of the American Revolution in which both Adams and Jenings were major participants.

Adams's letters speak for themselves and are, therefore, attended with little annotation, except that which indicates how they were "recycled," that is, how Adams included in them materials which he had already used in other connections, a common practice of the busy statesmen and letter writers of the period.

Contents

Introduction

AFTER THREE YEARS of distinguished service in the Continental Congress, John Adams was selected in the fall of 1777 to join Benjamin Franklin and Arthur Lee as a commissioner at the Court of Versailles. Adams arrived in France on April 1, 1778, and discovered that the principal business of his mission, the negotiation of treaties of amity and commerce, had already been accomplished. He found, nevertheless, plenty to occupy him in the French capital. Adams had been a regular writer in the American newspapers on the controversy with Great Britain and welcomed the invitation of Edmé Jacques Genet, the publisher of a newspaper controlled by the French Foreign Ministry—*Affaires de l'Angleterre et de l'Amérique*—to join Franklin and Lee as a contributor to his journal. As Genet explained to Adams, his "periodic work" belonged "entirely to the American cause and to Ms. les Députés." [1] From correspondence with Genet, it is clear that Adams produced an attack against the Carlisle Commission, a British embassy sent to the United States to propose reconciliation as an alternative to the French Alliance, and a proposal for French naval superiority on the coast of North America, but what else he wrote for *Affaires* before returning to America in June 1779 remains to be established (as docs the extent of Franklin's and Lee's contributions). [2]

Adams was back in Paris in February 1780, bearing a commission to negotiate peace with Great Britain. The French tried to discourage him from publicizing his mission for the good reason that news of it would solidify the position of Lord North's ministry by permitting it to claim that its uncompromising policies were driving the Americans to sue for peace. Adams, however, was determined to inform the British government and people of his powers. The only way to reach them was through the London newspapers. Someone with connections in the British newspaper world must be found to

---

[1] Genet to Adams, [1778?] (author's translation), Adams Papers microfilm, reel 349, Manuscript Division, Library of Congress.
[2] Genet to Adams, July 13, October 29, 1778, ibid.

serve as a conduit to the British public. Adams found his intermediary in Edmund Jenings.

Jenings is an intriguing figure. There are circumstances in his
career which arouse suspicions that he was a double agent, a servant
simultaneously of the British and American governments, who did
as much damage to the American cause as the more notorious prac-
titioner of duplicity Edward Bancroft. On the other hand, since the
evidence is indecisive and will support only inferences, one is reluc-
tant to point a finger at Jenings, lest injustice be done a man who
may well have been exactly what he and his friends represented him
to be: a gentleman "who has left his Affairs, from a Love to his
Country, to whose Service he devotes his Time." [3]

Jenings was born in Annapolis, Maryland, in 1731 to a well-to-do,
well-connected family. His father, attorney-general and secretary of
Maryland, was a first cousin of Thomas Lee of Stratford Hall, Virginia, father of the Lee brothers of revolutionary fame.[4] Sent to
England at an early age for his education—Eton, Cambridge, the
Middle Temple—Jenings apparently never returned to America,
but he carefully tended his Maryland and Virginia ties. In 1761 we
find him advising his cousin Arthur Lee to attend Edinburgh rather
than Oxford for a medical education.[5] In 1762 he vacationed for
six weeks at Tunbridge Wells with Charles Carroll of Carrollton.[6]
He lent money to prominent Virginia planters—Wormeley, Har-
rison, and Randolph (his brother-in-law)—and he augmented his
lands in Virginia and Maryland with occasional purchases. Having
inherited what served as the governor's mansion in Annapolis, Jenings sold it in 1768 to his friend Gov. Robert Eden, brother of
William Eden, head of the British Secret Service during the Revolutionary War.[7] During the late 1760s Jenings was admitted to mem-
bership in the Mississippi Company, a syndicate of Virginia and
Maryland land speculators seeking territory in the trans-Allegheny
region.[8]

---

[3] Adams to Franklin, April 19, 1780, ibid., reel 351.

[4] Ethel Armes, *Stratford Hall, the Great House of the Lees* (Richmond, Va.:
Garrett and Massie, 1936), p. 18.

[5] Arthur Lee to Richard Henry Lee, December 24–28, 1760, Lee Family Papers
microfilm, reel 1, Manuscript Division, Library of Congress.

[6] Charles Carroll to his father, November 11, 1762, Carroll Papers microfilm,
reel 1, Manuscript Division, Library of Congress.

[7] Jenings's moneylending and real estate transactions can be followed in detail
in Jenings Letterbook, 1753–1769, Virginia Historical Society, Richmond, Va.

[8] Jenings apparently became a member after December 1768; a list of members
as of that date does not contain his name. See Mann Butler, *A History of the*

In politics, Jenings was an admirer of William Pitt, whose portrait he presented, through Richard Henry Lee, to the gentlemen of Westmoreland County in 1768.[9] Since his material interests were involved in the quarrel between Britain and the colonies, Jenings closely monitored British political developments and cultivated a network of friendships among the politicians at Westminster. Like many of his contemporaries, he was caught up in the turbulence generated by the Stamp Act. He played an obscure role in obtaining for Zechariah Hood the appointment as Maryland stamp distributor,[10] which caused him to be stigmatized in Maryland and Virginia as a supporter of colonial taxation.[11] Jenings tried to efface this impression by shipping to the colonies an anonymous pamphlet which he had written against the Stamp Act and a print which he had "designed" to discredit it.[12] Unfavorable inferences about Jenings should not be drawn from his role in the Stamp Act crisis, for many other Americans, not the least of whom was Benjamin Franklin, were equally obtuse in not anticipating the depth of colonial opposition to parliamentary taxation.

The evidence is too thin to permit a description of Jenings's attitudes and activities between 1766 and 1776. In the latter year he may have written a pamphlet entitled *A Plan for Settling the Unhappy Dispute between Great Britain and Her Colonies.*[13] In 1778 and 1779 he wrote, anonymously, two more pamphlets, both of which censured British policy and recommended that the ministry accommodate American demands. One pamphlet he mentioned in his correspondence only as *Considerations.*[14] The other, *Twelve Letters on the Spirit and Resources of Great Britain,* published originally in London in Almon's *Remembrancer,* was reprinted in

---

Commonwealth of Kentucky (Louisville: Pub. for the author by Wilcox, Dickerman & Co., 1834), p. 383; Clarence W. Alvord and Clarence E. Carter, *The Critical Period, 1763–1765* (Springfield, Ill.: Trustees of the Illinois State Historical Library, 1915), pp 22–23.

[9] Jenings to Richard Henry Lee, November 1, 1768, *Virginia Historical Register and Literary Advertiser* 1 (1848): 73–74.

[10] Jenings to Price, February 28, 1766, Jenings Letterbook, 1753–1769; Jenings to Charles Carroll, May 27, 1766, Carroll Papers microfilm, reel 1: Thomas Hanley, *Charles Carroll of Carrollton: The Making of a Revolutionary Gentleman* (Washington: Catholic University of America Press, 1970), p. 211.

[11] Ibid., p. 211; Jenings to Robert Beverley, to Gawin Corbin, to John Taylor, April 2, 1766, Jenings Letterbook, 1753–1769.

[12] Jenings to Beverley, Corbin, Taylor, John Randolph, April 2, 1766, ibid.

[13] Joseph Sabin, *Bibliotheca Americana; a Dictionary of Books relating to America, from Its Discovery to the Present Time,* 29 vols. (New York, 1867–1936), 9:253.

[14] To Adams, March 10, 1779, Adams Papers microfilm, reel 350.

Philadelphia and Boston.[15] Jenings also wrote pro-American articles
for newspapers in London, Holland, and the Austrian Netherlands.[16]

For approximately a year, from September 1777 to September
1778, Jenings corresponded, over an array of pseudonyms, with
Arthur Lee, now American commissioner in Paris.[17] He supplied
information about British military and political movements, which
seemed to impress Lee, but which rarely rose above the common
gossip of the coffeehouse. Finally, Jenings served on a committee,
organized in December 1777, to collect money and distribute it to
American prisoners of war in British jails.[18]

Writing anti-British pamphlets, supplying information to the
American mission in Paris, relieving American prisoners of war—
what better credentials could a patriotic American have? Yet all of
these activities were used as covers by British agents. As for reviling
the British ministry in print and word, "tis an old practice," William
Lee observed, "for English spies to pretend the warmest Attachment
to the American Cause and to ridicule and abuse the Eng—h Ministry in all Companies." [19] Retailing "inside" information about
British operations was one of the ways that Bancroft, for example,
maintained his credibility with the American ministers at Paris.
And to gain the confidence of Franklin and his colleagues, more
than one scoundrel displayed solicitude for American prisoners—
the spy John Thornton, for example, who was Arthur Lee's secretary for a time, and Thomas Digges, a Maryland friend of Jenings
who also may have been a British spy.[20]

Still, what evidence is there that Jenings, while ostensibly serving
the American cause, was working for the British? He would, in the

---

[15] To Adams, April 25, 1779; Adams to Jenings, February 25, September 23,
1780, ibid., reels 350, 351 352. No copy of *Twelve Letters* appears to have sur-
vived.

[16] To Adams, February 19, March 5, 19, July 21, 1780, ibid., reels 351, 352.

[17] The letters are in the Lee Family Papers microfilm, reels 3 and 4, beginning
with Robert Williams [Jenings] to Arthur Lee, September 1, 1777. Jenings's
pseudonyms are listed in the introduction to the edition.

[18] Herbert E. Klingelhofer, "Matthew Ridley's Diary during the Peace Negotiations of 1782," *William and Mary Quarterly*, 3d. ser., 20 (1963): 95–96.

[19] William Lee to Edmé Genet, January 6, 1779, Genet Papers, 1778–1780,
Manuscript Division, Library of Congress.

[20] William Bell Clark does not refute the charge that Digges was a spy. That
confirmation of Digges's spying is absent from papers of some members of the
British ministry proves nothing. Only the discovery of the British Secret Service
papers after 1778 (discussed in the text, below) will exonerate or convict Digges.
Clark, "In Defense of Thomas Digges," *Pennsylvania Magazine of History and
Biography* 77 (1953): 381–438.

first place, have had an economic incentive to be a double agent. He held large properties in both Britain and America, which were jeopardized by the civil war within the empire.[21] Were he to be identified as a conspicuous partisan of one country, the other might confiscate his holdings (as Maryland did, on the grounds that he was a British subject; evidence of his services to the United States caused the state to reverse itself later). One way to save his estates in both countries was to do—or appear to do—the bidding of both. He was, moreover, always concerned that his loyalty to the United States was about to be challenged. "When I make this offer [of assistance]," he wrote Adams on February 19, 1780, "I assure myself you are satisfied of my Fidelity & Affection to my Country." [22] Since Adams never doubted Jenings's loyalty, Jenings's anxiety about its being suspect suggests that he may have been engaged in disloyal acts. More compromising is a letter of British spymaster John Vardill showing Jenings in London in 1778 shuttling with letters between Britain's most effective spies in the American camp in Paris, Bancroft and Van Zandt (alias George Lupton).[23] Jenings's connection with Bancroft was, in fact, an enduring one, for in the summer of 1783 he wrote and sent to America, "under the patronage . . . of Doctor Bancroft," a pamphlet defending himself against charges of disloyalty to the United States.[24] Finally, there is the affair of the "Anonymous Letters."

Late in 1782 Henry Laurens accused Jenings of having written and widely circulated an anonymous letter, dated May 3, 1782, in which Adams was assailed for having "laboured clandestinely in injuring Franklin and Laurens." [25] Laurens, moreover, was cer-

---

21 It is difficult to estimate the value of Jenings's real property and money at interest in America. One revealing comment is that in 1757 Jenings believed the interest due him on loans outstanding in Virginia was "greatly" is excess of £1700 sterling. In 1766 he admitted to his sister that "it is imagined indeed I am worth a great deal." What the value of his holdings were by 1776 it is impossible to determine. In England Jenings owned large estates and rental properties in Yorkshire. Jenings to Ariana Randolph, November 24, 1757, 1766; to Richard Corbin, April 25, 1757; to Mr. Reynard, April 24, 1759, Jenings Letterbook, 1753–1769.

22 Adams Papers microfilm, reel 351.

23 Vardill to William Eden, December 22, 1777, in Benjamin F. Stevens, *B. F. Stevens's Facsimiles of Manuscripts in European Archives Relating to America, 1773–1783*, 24 portfolios (London: Photographed and printed by Malby & Sons, 1889–95), portfolio 2, no. 232.

24 Henry Laurens to Robert Livingston, September 11, 1783, Papers of the Continental Congress microfilm, reel 117, National Archives and Records Service.

25 Edmund Jenings, *The Candor of Henry Laurens, Esq; Manifested by his*

tain—"as sure the performance was his as I could be sure of his
hand-writing"—that Jenings had written another anonymous letter,
January 31, 1782, to Franklin in which Adams was represented as
having abused Franklin and was declared "wholly unfit" for his
diplomatic position in the Netherlands. The American cause in
Holland could only be saved, it was alleged, if Franklin assumed its
management.[26] Care was taken that both Adams and Franklin received a copy of this letter, as the principals had of that of May 3.

Jenings vehemently denied that he had written either letter, but
in rebutting Laurens's charge he was caught up in a flagrant falsehood, which convinced Laurens that his disavowal was altogether
mendacious, that he was a "traitor" to the American cause whose
"chief business has been to create dissentions" among the commis-
sioners, and that "he has been the principal contriver and manager
of Anonymous Letters calculated for that purpose." [27] Trafficking in
abusive, anonymous letters was not, in fact, out of character for
Jenings. He had sent Adams one such missive on November 14, 1781,
in which Adams was traduced by a Frenchman whom he assumed to
be the comte de Vergennes.[28] But whether Jenings fabricated this
and the other letters, which indisputably created hard feelings
among the American ministers, and whether he was the traitorous
villain Laurens assumed him to be can only be established if the
major documentary gap in the writing of the diplomacy of the
Revolution—the absence of the British Secret Service papers from
the winter of 1778 until the end of the war—is filled during this
Bicentennial period.

For as long as William Eden ran the Secret Service, its papers exist
in the rich profusion which we find duplicated in Stevens's *Facsimiles*. But in the winter of 1778 Eden was appointed to the Carlisle Commission and sent to America. Who succeeded him as
overseer of American espionage and where the papers generated by

---

Behaviour to Mr. Edmund Jenings (London, 1783), p. 5, Rare Book and Special
Collections Division, Library of Congress. The letter appears in the Adams Papers
under the date of June 6, 1782.

[26] Henry Laurens, *Mr. Laurens's True State of the Case. By Which His Candor
to Mr. Edmund Jenings Is Manifested, and the Tricks of Mr. Jenings Are Detected* (London, 1783), pp. 28–29, Rare Book and Special Collections Division,
Library of Congress. The letter appears in the Adams Papers as WR to Franklin,
January 31, 1782, microfilm, reel 356.

[27] Henry Laurens to Robert Livingston, September 11, 1783, Papers of the
Continental Congress microfilm, reel 117.

[28] Jenings to Adams, November 14, 1781, Adams Family Papers microfilm, reel
355.

the effort are—if, in fact, they exist—is unknown. That spying on American diplomats in Europe continued after Eden's departure is certain, because records indicate that Bancroft continued to be paid for his work until the war's end.[29] If Jenings was a British agent, the accomplishment of George III's Secret Service is even more impressive than previously supposed, for it would have succeeded in planting spies in the highest councils of every major American diplomat: Bancroft as Franklin's secretary; John Thornton and Hezekiah Ford as Lee's secretaries; William Carmichael, a fellow Marylander and friend of Jenings, as Jay's secretary,[30] and Jenings himself as Adams's advisor and confidant. Confirmation of such a feat awaits, however, the discovery of the Secret Service documents.

For now, Jenings must remain an enigma. There is even a mystery about when Adams and he first met. The editors of the Adams Papers assume that the two men met in Paris in April 1778, soon after Adams arrived in France, but Jenings was in London at the time.[31] He apparently stayed there until September 1778 and crossed over to Paris in October.[32] He and Adams must have become acquainted between October 1778 and the beginning of March 1779, when the latter left Paris for America. When Adams returned to France in the winter of 1780, Jenings had taken up residence in Brussels, where he lived, when not visiting Adams and other American diplomats, until he returned permanently to England in the winter of 1783.

The basis of the friendship between Adams and Jenings is, characteristically, subject to two interpretations. The bond between

---

29 Bancroft to Carmarthen, September 16, 1784, Foreign Office 4:3, Public Record Office, London; photostat in Manuscript Division, Library of Congress.

30 For allegations of Carmichael's disloyalty, see John Jay, *John Jay, the Making of a Revolutionary*, ed. Richard B. Morris, vol. 1 (New York: Harper & Row, 1975), pp. 770–71. I am not convinced that Carmichael was a spy, although until his career can be clarified he remains a rather equivocal character.

31 See John Adams, *The Diary and Autobiography of John Adams*, ed. Lyman H. Butterfield, 4 vols. (Cambridge: Harvard University Press, 1961), 2:355–56. The Adams Papers editors base their assumption on a letter, April 20, 1778, from John Adams to an addressee identified, apparently by Adams in his old age, as Jenings. But Adams could not have known Jenings at the time, for Jenings was living in London, as his letters to Lee from the British capital of May 1, 12, 19, 1778, attest. Lee Family Papers microfilm, reel 4.

32 See Jenings to Arthur Lee, post September 26, 1778, ibid., reel 5. The first reference to Jenings in Paris which I have found is slightly ambiguous but seems to establish his presence in the French capital in October 1778. Edmé Genet to Adams, October 29, 1778, Adams Papers microfilm, reel 349. For a reference to Jenings in Paris in December 1778, see Matthew Ridley to Edmé Genet, December 20, 1778, Genet Papers, 1778–1780.

them may have been intellectual compatibility: "as far as I can Judge of your Sentiments, mine are entirely conformable to them," wrote Jenings to Adams on March 10, 1779.[33] Or, Jenings may have capitalized on what Adams's critics in Congress feared was his special vulnerability, his vanity;[34] that is, by gratifying Adams's immoderate vanity, Jenings may have flattered himself into his favor.

Adams in France was an easy mark for a flatterer, for his pride had been humbled and he was without friends. The French treated him like a very small fish: "it being settled that he was not the famous Adams, the consequence was plain," he bitterly confided to his diary, that "he was some Man nobody had ever heard of before—and therefore a man of no Consequence—a Cypher."[35] Adams's reluctance to participate in the quarrels of Franklin and Lee and their satellites left him, he felt, as an outcast: "there is no man here [in Paris] that I dare trust at present," he wrote on February 9, 1779.[36] In this situation a little attention, a few kind words, would go a long way. Whether Jenings perceived this and laid his plans accordingly or whether his natural manner ran toward flattery, he complimented Adams shamelessly. On April 25, 1779, in the second letter he wrote to Adams, he rhapsodized: "the great Part you have taken in the American Question & your Judgment in it, are such as give you a right to Influence & direct every One interested in the Event. . . . I have many reasons to make me wish your staying here, where I think disinterested Men are more wanted than in America. . . . the more of Trust & Knowledge, that are here, the better it will be to prevent any Mischievous Consequences."[37] Jenings's next letter was in the same style: "You have put your Hand to the Plough & must not look back nor do I think ought any of those great Men, who have hitherto laboured in the field."[38] And so were his subsequent ones.

Whether Jenings seduced Adams with flattery—Laurens suspected so, for he lamented Adams's being under the "fascination" of Jenings[39]—or whether they found in each other an honest meeting of the minds, their friendship was exceedingly close. The letters passing between them from 1780 to 1783 are surpassed in volume only

---

[33] Adams Papers microfilm, reel 350.
[34] Elbridge Gerry to Adams, February 24, 1785, ibid., reel 364.
[35] Entry of February 11, 1779, in *Adams, Diary and Autobiography*, 2:351.
[36] Ibid., p. 347.
[37] Adams Papers microfilm, reel 350.
[38] May 25, 1779, ibid.
[39] Laurens, *Mr. Laurens's True State of the Case*, p. 67.

by those exchanged by Adams and his wife. Adams trusted Jenings implicitly, recommending him for numerous positions—including secretary to the American peace commission in 1782 [40]—and vindicating him against all imputations of disloyalty. "I believe you as innocent of it, as an Angel in Heaven," he assured Jenings on May 13, 1784.[41] Jenings was nothing less than Adams's best friend in Europe. "In all Events," wrote Adams on April 18, 1783, "don't let You & me be caught in any snare. I have never had many intimate Friends, and I am not disposed to part with one easily." [42]

No little part of Jenings's value to Adams was his connections in the British publishing world, connections which Adams began exploiting, as has already been said, when he returned to France as peace negotiator in 1780. In his correspondence with Adams, Jenings never revealed how he was able to place American writings in the London newspapers. He speaks only of his correspondents, of his friends, who may have been the newspaper publishers themselves or intermediaries who had influence with them. One thing is certain: Jenings had a particularly good pipeline to what the French considered "the most renouned" gazette of the opposition, "le general advertiser imprimé par Mr. Parker." [43] William Parker, publisher of *The General Advertiser and Morning Intelligencer*,[44] was a virulent opponent of the British ministry (as most London newspaper editors of the day were), who in 1780 was editing his paper from Newgate, where he had been committed for contempt of the House of Lords.[45] On April 2, 1780, Adams asked Jenings "to have some Paragraphs inserted in the English Newspapers, announcing the Purport of my Mission." [46] Jenings promptly inserted an announcement in the *General Advertiser* (April 12–13) and continued to scatter through its pages the steady diet of materials which Adams furnished him. An account, for example, of Adams's travels in Spain, on his way to assume his position in France, was published (May 1), as were Adams's strictures over the signature of Probus (a pseudonym supplied, characteristically, by Jenings) on speeches by Henry Seymour

---

[40] Adams to Franklin, April 19, 1780; to President of Congress, May 16, 1782; to Laurens, August 15, 1782; Adams Papers microfilm, reels 351, 106 107.

[41] Ibid., reel 107.

[42] Ibid., reel 108.

[43] Edmé Genet to Adams, February 25, 1780, ibid., reel 351.

[44] The prefix *Parker's* was added in 1782.

[45] Solomon Lutnick, *The American Revolution and the British Press, 1775–1783* (Columbia, Mo.: University of Missouri Press, 1967), pp. 12–14, 33.

[46] Adams to Jenings, April 2, 1780, Adams Papers microfilm, reel 351.

Conway and Lord George Germaine.[47]

On May 16, 1780, Thomas Digges, who had been writing Adams from London under a variety of pseudonyms, sent him a number of pamphlets written by Joseph Galloway, with whom Adams had served in the First Continental Congress but who was now the leading Loyalist pamphleteer in Britain.[48] Although he held Galloway in contempt—"a meaner, falser heart never circulated blood" [49]— Adams was evidently struck by the force of one of the pamphlets in Digges's consignment—*Cool Thoughts on the Consequences to Great Britain of American Independence*—and decided to write an answer to it, in which he would turn Galloway's arguments in opposition to American independence on their head.[50] From late June through the middle of July Adams wrote at least twelve essays in answer to *Cool Thoughts*, sending them to Jenings in installments. Jennings apparently received the final section by July 27, 1780.[51]

Jenings immediately perceived the essays' significance; "they are of such Importance," he wrote Adams on July 27, "that I shall be careful to whom they are trusted & therefore may perhaps wait a little while, before I find a convenient opportunity" to send them to England.[52] The essays apparently reached London in good order, but publication was not forthcoming. "What is become of the Remarks upon Galloway?" Adams wrote Jenings on February 11, 1781.[53] This query produced no results and Adams did not pursue the matter further. But he did not forget the essays. "Pray what has become of them," he wrote Jenings on July 17, 1782; "Can you get them back? I shall be very glad to see them again. Since they are not worth printing in London, I would have them published here in French." [54] Replied Jenings on August 11, 1782: "the Person to

---

[47] The extracts from the *General Advertiser* appear in the Adams Papers microfilm, reel 351, under the date of April 5, 1780; see also Jenings to Adams, July 9, 1780; ibid., reel 352.

[48] Alexander Brett [Digges] to Adams, June 8, 1780, ibid., reel 351.

[49] Adams to Jenings, July 16, 1780, ibid., reel 352.

[50] Adams suspected that *Cool Thoughts* was produced by several American Loyalists in concert wth Galloway, "given out as the ostensible as he probably was the principal Author." To the President of Congress, June 16, 17, 1780, ibid., reel 100.

[51] Jenings to Adams, July 9, 21, 27, 1780; Adams to Jenings, July 18, 22, 1780; ibid., reel 352.

[52] Jenings to Adams, July 27, 1780, ibid.

[53] Ibid., reel 354.

[54] Ibid., reel 357.

whom I sent some time ago the answer to Galloway is very idle or
very busy. I have written him several times to publish it." To which
he added on August 22, 1782: "something will be done with the
long lost performance. I wish they may be published to your Excellency's satisfaction. It is to be looked for in the General Advertiser."[55]

On August 23, 1782, the *General Advertiser* published the first of
the "lost" essays; nine more followed at intervals, the last appearing
in the December 26, 1782, issue. The essays were attributed to a
"Distinguished American" and were given false dates, making it
appear that they were written between January 17 and February 6,
1782. In attributing the essays to an American, the publisher of the
General Advertiser played havoc with the pronouns. "They were
written," Adams informed Jenings, "with the Design of being
printed as written by a Briton. The publisher has told that they are
of an American! Which makes the We's Us's etc very odd. They will
think them from a Penitent Refugee." [56]

The force and penetration of the essays were so apparent that no
sooner had they begun appearing than a demand arose for a reprint-
ing. "I find it is the wish of some to see the letters now publishing
in the newspapers collected in a Pamphlet," wrote Jenings to Adams
on September 25, 1782.[57] Adams consented to a pamphlet edition,
but left the editing and arrangements to Jenings. With the prospect
of joining the peace negotiations at Paris before him, he did not,
he told his friend, "have the Time to meddle with" the writings.[58]

In June 1783, some months after the negotiations were concluded,
Adams turned his attention to the essays, for he regarded them as
having adumbrated the terms of the preliminary peace. "There are
in those letters so many of the characteristick features of the Provisional Treaty of 30th Nov. 1782," he wrote Robert Livingston on
June 9, 1783, "that the publication of them in England at the time
when they appeared may be supposed to have contributed more or
less to propogate such Sentiments. . . . And as they were written by
one of your ministers at the Conference of Peace, who repeated &
extended the same Arguments to the British Ministers in the Course
of the Negotiations, it is proper that you should be informed of
them.[59]

---

[55] Ibid.
[56] Adams to Jenings, September 16, 1782, ibid., reel 358.
[57] Ibid.
[58] Adams to Jenings, September 27, 1782, ibid., reel 358.
[59] Adams to Robert Livingston, June 9, 1783, ibid., reel 108.

Collecting the essays for publication posed unexpected difficulties. Adams complained that he had "committed a great indiscretion in sending them in the year 1780 from Paris without keeping a Copy of a single line of them." [60] Could Jenings retrieve them? Jenings could not oblige Adams, because the manuscript copies had been cut up and handed to different compositors, "the mode of setting things for the Press requiring that it should be cut into Pieces for the distribution of them into several hands at a time. . . ." [61] He did manage to recover and return two essays which had not been printed. These survive among Adams's manuscripts.

The disappearance of most of the original essays frustrated Adams's desire to see the whole series printed in a "complete Publication." [62] After a while he forgot about them. As a result, they were never reprinted.[63] Until now, therefore, this important series has remained unknown and inaccessible to students of the Revolution.

---

[60] Adams to Cerisier, June 9, 1783, ibid., reel 361.

[61] Jenings, to Adams, June, 1783, ibid., reel 361.

[62] Adams to Jenings, June 9, 1783, ibid., reel 108.

[63] Parts of the Distinguished American letters were printed, in French, in *Le Politique hollandais*, an American journal published by one Antoine Cerisier. Adams's contributions to *Le Politique hollandais* have not been identified, but they must have been extensive, for one of Franklin's correspondents informed the doctor that "others as well as myself almost from the first appearance of the Politique Hollandais heard it as no secret that all that concerned America in that Paper was literally translated from his [Adams's] own writings," a fact which Adams confirmed in a letter of May 16, 1782, to Congress. Adams's contributions, spread through French papers like the *Mercure de Paris* and Dutch papers like the *Gazette de Leide*, also await identification, as do the newspaper writings of Lee, Franklin, and other American diplomats in Europe. See Adams to Cerisier, June 9, 1783; WR to Franklin, January 31, 1782; Adams to Congress, May 16, 1782; ibid., reels 108, 356, 106.

LETTERS
from a
Distinguished
American

LETTER I

Parker's General Advertiser and Morning Intelligencer
August 23, 1782

SIR, *Paris, Jan. 17, 1782.*

I have not till lately obtained a sight of a number of Pamphlets, ascribed indeed to Mr. Galloway but containing the mention of such circumstances, as convince me that they were written in concert between the American Refugees and the British Ministry. In some of them I perceive apparently unequivocal traces of the hand of the late Governor Hutchinson. I have read them with surprize, because it seems to me, that if their professed intention had been to convince America, that it is both her interest and duty to support her Sovereignty and her Alliances,[1] and the interest and duty of all the maritime powers of Europe to support her in them, the writers could not have taken methods more effectual.

The Author of the "Cool Thoughts on the Consequences of American Independence" observes, that "an offensive and defensive alliance between France and America will naturally coinside with their several views and interests, as soon as American Independence shall be acknowledged by the powers in Europe. America will naturally wish, while she is rising from her infant state into opulence and power, to cover her dominions under the protection of France; and France will find new resources of strength in American commerce, armies, and naval force. The recovery of America, from the disasters and distresses of war, will be rapid and sudden; very

---

[1] This phrase, beginning with *because*, is incorporated directly from Adams's letter to Congress of June 16, 1780. This letter and two of June 17, 1780, to Congress he used both as outlines and as sources of material for the Distinguished American essays. Borrowings will be noted as they occur. See Adams to the president of Congress, June 16, 1780, in U.S. Department of State, *The Revolutionary Diplomatic Correspondence of the United States*, ed. Francis Wharton, 6 vols. (Washington: Government Printing Office, 1889), 3:788.

unlike an old country, whose population is full, and whose cultivation, commerce, and strength have arrived at their height. The multiplication of her numbers, and the increase of her power, will surpass all expectation. If her sudden growth has already exceeded the most sanguine ideas, it is certain, that the increase of her strength, when supported and assisted by France, and pushed forward by the powerful motives, arising from her separate interest, her own preservation, and the prospect of her own rising glory and importance among nations, will far out-run any idea we have had of her late population."

It is pleasing to see the irresistible force of truth operating upon the minds even of the most inveterate and disingenuous of the enemies of America. It was impossible to deny, that the alliance between France and the United States is natural, and founded on their mutual interests. It was impossible to deny, that the resurrection of America from the distresses of this war will be sudden and surprising. But *is this an argument for England to continue the war?* Will the resurrection of England out of the ruins of this war be *sudden?* If she continues it much longer, will she ever arise *again?* The present and future state of Great Britain, then, are decisive argument (if reason could be heard) for making peace immediately: while the present and future state of America are arguments equally unanswerable for America to continue the war, until her Independence shall be acknowledged by all the world. It is equally an argument for France and Spain, and Holland, to exert themselves to support American Independence, because, by this means they will effectively secure her gratitude and good will: they will bind the connections between them the closer, and the sudden rise of America out of her distresses into affluence and power, will enable her to repay those nations whatever debts may be contracted, and to become an able ally to defend them in case of need against their enemies; or, if the true American system of policy should be peace and neutrality, as no doubt it will, they will derive such commerce and naval supplies from America for ever, hereafter, as will secure them the freedom of the seas. This is also a powerful motive for all the maritime nations of Europe to favour and support American Independence. It is the true interest of all the maritime nations, that America should have a free trade with all of them, and that she should be neutral in all their wars. Every body now throughout the world sees, that a renewal of the English monopoly of the American trade, would establish an absolute tyranny upon the ocean, and that every other ship that sails would hold its liberty at the mercy of these Lordly Islanders. If the French or Spaniards were to obtain a monopoly of this trade, it would give them a superiority over all the other commercial nations, which would be dangerous to the freedom of navigators. It is obviously then the interest and duty of all the maritime powers to keep the American trade open and free to all, and to be sure to prevent its being monopolized by any one nation whatever. Another inference that may fairly and must ———— [line missing in text] America will suddenly arise out of the distresses of the war to affluence and power, is this:—That all the monied men in Europe ought to transfer as fast as possible their stocks from British to American funds: For as it is certain, that England will not suddenly rise out of the disasters of the war, and it is at least dubious whether she will ever rise out of them; the interest neither of the capitalist, nor the speculator, is safe in the English funds; whereas, whatever money may be lent to America, is safe and sure, both for principal and interest, and it will become easier every day for America to pay both.

Thus it appears, that Mr. Galloway is involuntarily forced to lay open truths, which supports her credit, and unites the interests of all the world in her favour against Great Britain.

This writer goes on: "Nor will it be the interest of America to check the ambition of France, while confined to Europe. Her distance, and the safety arising from it, will render her regardless of the fate of nations, on this side of the Atlantic, as soon as her own strength shall be established. The prosperity or ruin of kingdoms, from whose power they can have nothing to fear, and whose alliance they can never want, will be matters of equal indifference. She can wish for no other connection with Europe, than that of commerce; and this will be better secured in the hands of an ally, than in those with whom she holds other connections; so that it will be of little moment to her, whether Great Britain, Spain, Holland, Germany, or Russia, shall be ruled by one or more Monarchs."

Here again it is manifest, that this gentleman clearly sees her true interest and political system, in relation to Europe, and the true interest and political system of all Europe towards America. *Both consist in two words, peace and commerce.* It can never, after the conclusion of the war, and the final establishment of the independence of America, be her interest to go to war with any nation of Europe; and it can never be the interest of any one of the maritime powers to go to war with her, unless we should except Great

Britain, and there is no sufficient reason, perhaps, for excepting her. It is not improbable, however, that the selfish, unsocial tyrannical spirit, which has hitherto dictated to her the maxim of making war with every nation, that has commerce and a considerable marine, may still prompt her to endeavour to destroy the navy of America. If it should, however, she will not succeed, and will only ruin herself by it.

But if it will not be the interest of America to go to war with any power of Europe, it will certainly be her interest to trade with every power of Europe, because the greater number and variety of markets are open to her, the greater will be the demand for her productions, the greater quantity of them she will sell, and she will obtain so much a better price, and the cheaper and easier will she obtain the commodities of the growth, production and manufacture of Europe that she wants. On the contrary, if it is not the interest of any nation of Europe to go to war with her, it will be the interest of every one of them to trade with her, because she has commodities that every one of them wants, and every one of them has commodities that she wants; so that a barter may be carried on advantageous on all sides; and, besides this, every maritime power in Europe must endeavour to have a share in American commerce, in order to maintain her share of the commerce of Europe, to maintain her marine upon a proportional footing, and maintain her rank among the other maritime powers.

This observation then, instead of being an argument for any one to continue the war, is a very forcible one to shew the danger to the other powers of Europe, arising from the former connection between America and England; and also to shew, that the other maritime powers ought to interfere in assisting America to maintain her independence, and also to maintain her true system of neutrality in future, that the blessings of her commerce may be open to all. As to the idea of the ambition of France, for universal monarchy, it is a chimera, fit to amuse the madness of Britains, which in this moment catches at any thing, however extravagant, to plague and harass herself with. But it is fit for the rest of the world to smile at. Universal Monarchy at land is impracticable; but universal Monarchy at sea has been well nigh established, and would before this moment have been perfected, if Great Britain and America had continued united. France can never entertain an hope of it, unless the fury of Great Britain should be assisted by the folly, the indolence, and inactivity of the other maritime powers, so as to drive the American commerce wholly into the hands of France, which is not to be supposed; but, on the contrary, every trading nation will, no doubt, demand a share in American trade, and will consequently augment their riches and naval power in proportion.

LETTER II

Parker's General Advertiser and Morning Intelligencer
August 27, 1782

SIR,   *Paris, Jan. 28, 1782.*
   Every American will agree with the writer on the consequence of American Independence, that the United States, when their Independence shall be no longer disputed, can wish for no other connection with Europe than that of commerce. No good American would wish to involve his country in the labyrinths of European negotiations, or in the iniquities of their wars. America will wish to be a common blessing to all the nations of Europe, without injuring any; and such will be her demand for the productions of each of them, that each one will derive material advantages in the increase of the means of subsistence, and consequent population, from supplying her wants. Each of them wants her commodities in exchange, and no one of them can reasonably wish to cramp the growth, and prevent the happiness of the human species in both worlds, by confining the advantages of this commerce to itself.
   It is equally clear, that this commerce will be better secured by her own wisdom, than by the domination of any European power; and safer in the hands of an ally than a master. But it is amazing that this man's malice against his native country should have suffered such important truths in her favour to escape him. It shews that he knows not how to conduct the cause he patronized, and that he is wrong headed, as he is malicious and insidious.
   "The new states are, and will continue the allies of France, our natural enemy, unless reduced." England ought to consider, whether

all attempts to reduce the new States have not a tendency to rivet
the alliance with France, and to drive the States to the necessity
of forming closer connections with her than they have now; to
make all America too the natural enemy of England for ever; to
drive her to more rigorous renunciations of British trade; nay, to
a final and total prohibition of it; to enter into engagements with
France, Spain, Holland, and other maritime powers, to this effect.
It ought to be considered, whether, the new States will not become
soon the allies of Spain too, and continue so for ever, If this war
is pursued much farther. As to reducing these States, the idea of it,
at this day, is fit only for ridicule and contempt. It is derided in
every town in America. This country will never again be in quiet
and continual possession of one State of the thirteen, not even of
Georgia. South Carolina, where we are melting into disease and
death that army which ought to be defending the West India
Islands, will never be ours a single month; no, not for an hour.

This writer goes on, "The far greater part of the people wish
and hope for an union with this country." It is not possible to
conceive any thing more barefacedly false than this. A Germain,
or a Conway may be excused, on account of ignorance and mis-
information; but this man knows better than he says. But having
forfeited his life to the laws of his country, and by the black cata-
logue of his crimes, rendered himself unpardonable, he has vowed
to revenge himself, not like Coriolanus, by his sword, but by mis-
representations.

But he adds, "the greater part of the people are ready to unite
with the King's forces, in reducing the power of their tyrants," by
which he means, no doubt, the Congress and the new government.
Nothing can shew the complection of this assertion better than to
recollect the orders which are constantly given by the Commanding
Officers in New York, which are published in the newspapers. They
dare not trust the Provincials and Volunteers, and Militia, &c. as
they call them, of whom such an ostentatious parade is made in the
dispatches of Commanding Officers and Court Gazettes. They exercise them in the day time with bits of wood in their musquets for
flints; they take the arms from them every night, and pile them in
the magazines; and they forbid them to be trusted with any quantity
of powder. The truth is, the only consequence that the Com-
manders of the English troops have found, in giving arms and
cloathing and ammunition to any of the inhabitants, whenever
they have been, has been to cloath, arm, and supply their expenses.

General Burgoyne found it so in New England, and New York. General Howe found it so in New Jersey, Pennsylvania, Maryland, and Delaware; and Sir Henry Clinton and Earl Cornwallis found it so in Georgia and South Carolina. What encouragement could have been given that has not? Is exemption from plunder encouragement? Forbid plunder, and half your army will desert; nay, for the provisions, horses, cattle, you take, you enrich the country with English guineas, and enable the people to buy arms, ammunition, cloathing, and every thing they want from your own soldiers. By large bounties, and by commissions, a few banditti, who have no honour nor principle to bind them to any country, or any cause, may be collected, but these would betray their new masters the first opportunity, and will be very few in number. The great body of the people in every state revere the Congress, more sincerely, than British soldiers revere their . . . . They reverence it as the voice of their country, the guardians of its right, and the voice of God; and they esteem their Independence and alliance with France, as the two greatest blessings which providence ever yet bestowed upon the new world. They think them equal blessings to Europe in general, as to America; and are universally of opinion, that a Council of Statesmen consulting for their good, and the good of mankind, could not have devised a plan, so much for their honour, interest, liberty and happiness, as that which has been derived, by the folly and imprudence of Great Britain. He goes on, "the treachery of this country, in not exerting its powers for their relief, will create permanent resentment." How many lives, and how many millions, has this country already sacrificed? Probably more lives, certainly more millions than the whole of the last war cost us. What was the fruit of the last war? Triumph and conquest by sea and land in every part of the world. What the effect of this? Defeat, disgrace, loss of America, West India Islands, African, Mediterranean, and German and Holland trade, the contempt of all nations, the Independence of Ireland, and a civil war in England; yet the war is to be continued!

"Gratitude to the nations which shall save them from our ravages, will stamp impressions never to be effaced." Stop the ravages then; and the further gratitude and impressions will be prevented. "Further Treaties of Alliance and Commerce will be made." No longer war, no further Treaties. This can only be the effect of British imprudence. The treaties already made are well known. What further treaties Ministry may drive them to, will depend upon themselves.

With the Independence of America, we must give up our fisheries
"on the banks of Newfoundland and in the American seas." Sup-
posing this true, which it is not at present, but our infatuation in
continuing the war may make it so, what follows? If Britain lose
them, who will gain them? France and America. Have not France
and America then as urgent a motive to contend for the gain, as
we to prevent the loss? Are they not an object as important and
desirable to France and America, as to us? Have they not as much
reason to fight for them, as England? Will they easily give up the
Independence of America, which is to bear such tempting fruit?
One would think this writer was in the interest of France and
America still, and labouring to persuade them, that they are fight-
ing for a rich and a glorious prize. The question then is reduced to
another, viz. which[2] has the best prospect of contending for them
successfully—America, France and Spain, favoured by all the world,
or England, thwarted and opposed by all the world? And to whom
did God and Nature give them? Ministry lay great stress upon the
gift of God and Nature, when they consider the advantages of our
insular situation, to justify their injustice and hostility against all
the maritime powers. Why should Americans hold the blessings of
Providence in a baser estimation, which they can enjoy, without
injury to any nation whatever.

"With American Independence, says he, we must give up thirty-
five thousand American seamen, and twenty-eight thousand more,
bred and maintained in those excellent nurseries, the fisheries. Our
valuable trade, carried on from thence with the Roman Catholic
States, will be in the hands of America. These nurseries, and this
trade, will ever remain the natural right of the people, who inhabit
that country. A trade so profitable, and a nursery of seamen so
excellent, and so necessary for the support of her naval force, will
never be given up, or even divided by America with any power
whatsoever."

If all this were true, what then? If Britain loses it all, by American Independence, who will gain it? These advantages are not to
be lost out of the world. Who will find them, but America and
France? These are the powers at war, for these very objects, if they
are the necessary consequences of American Independence, will they
not fight as bravely to obtain them, as the English? It is here
admitted they are the natural rights of America, will not she con-

---

[2] For the material from here to the end of the paragraph, see Adams to
the president of Congress, June 16, 1780, ibid., p. 789.

tend for it? Who then has the most power, one nation or three? Perhaps five or six before the end? Are 60,000 seamen a feebler bulwark for America or France, than for England? Are they feebler instruments of wealth, power and glory, in the service of America, than England? At the command of Congress, than the Kings? [3] The question occurs then, who is the strongest? However, we need not lose so many seamen, nor the fishery, nor the trade with Roman Catholick countries, by American Independence. America never thought of excluding England from the fishery, and the profits of her trade to Roman Catholick countries would again, be useful to England, and center here, if peace were made now. But let it be remembered, America grows every day of this war more independent of England for manufactures, by the amazing increase of her own; and France, Spain, and even the states of Italy and Germany, and *Ireland too,* are every day putting themselves more and more in a condition to supply America; so that every day of the continuance of this ruinous war, increases the facility and the inclinations of America to supply herself elsewhere, and the capacity of other nations to supply her, and of consequences makes it more and more inevitable for England to lose the seamen, the fisheries, and the trade. The question recurs at every sentence, who is the ablest to hold out? America, that grows stronger every year, and that too in ways and degrees that England has no idea of, or England that grows weaker? But England's misfortune and ruin are, that *it never knew America,* nor her resources, nor the character of her people.

---

[3] For this and the two preceding sentences, see ibid., p. 789.

LETTER III

Parker's General Advertiser and Morning Intelligencer
August 30, 1782

SIR,   *Paris, January 29, 1782.*
The Writer on the Consequences of American Independence adds,
"the British Islands in the West Indies must fall of course. The
same power that can compel Great Britain to yield up America,
will compel her to give up the West Indies. They are evidently the
immediate objects of France."

It is very true, that if we continue the war, the West Indies must
fall into the hands of France. England has held them by no other
tenure, than the courtesy of France and Spain, for two years past.
Britons, be not deceived! You can defend these islands only by your
Navy, and the friendship of North America. Your Navy was not
what it was the last war. The loss of America has put it out of your
power, for ever, until your regain the friendship of America, and a
share of her trade, to have such a Navy, as you once had. Your
ships are weak and unable to sustain the shocks of winds, and seas,
and battles, as formerly. The masts and spars are not to be depended
on as heretofore. The rigging, notwithstanding the immense sums
granted for the sea service, is not as it was. Your ships are not
manned, as they were, either in the numbers or qualities of the
seamen. Your Officers then have not the same dependence upon
ships, spars, rigging, or men, which they had in former wars, and
consequently cannot perform what they once could.

The Navies of your enemies are as far from being what they once
were. They are as much improved, as your's are declined. It is
also now plain, from a vast number of experiments, that the science
of naval tacticks is now quite as well understood, and all the
manoeuvers as ably executed by the French Officers as by the English. Add to this, the advantages that the French and Spanish fleets
and armies have over the English, in the supplies of provisions,

artificers, and materials, which they now draw from the United States of North America, and every man must see, that we hold these Islands at the mere mercy of our enemies, and if we continue this war, we shall infallibly lose them. Our policy is plain then: "Let us make peace, while these Islands are our's, and America will never be obliged, nor inclined, in any future war, to assist France in attaining them, as they are now bound to do by treaty, while this war continues. North America, it is plain, will never wish to govern these Islands. The reason is obvious: they will be as profitable to her as under the government of France, Spain or England, as they could be under her own, and she will be at no expense to protect, secure, or defend them."

If the British West Indies Islands should be taken by France and Spain, how are we to recover them at the peace? What have we taken, to exchange for them? What are we likely to take?

"Our only true policy is, to make peace, and save the Islands while we may." Once taken, it will be more difficult to recover them. Are we able to keep peace at home, in Ireland, in the East Indies, and with the neutral maritime powers, who have unanimously declared against us, as clearly, as if they had declared war in favour of America; and continue the war long enough to annihilate the fleets of France and Spain, retake our lost Islands, and after that reduce the United States of America to submission? For these stubborn spirits will remain to be reduced, after France and Spain shall be beaten. Will our soldiers, seamen, and revenues, never fail till this is done? How many more years of war will this cost us? And after all these miraculous feats shall be accomplished, will our resources enable us to maintain a sufficient force to keep down the power of France, Spain, and America? We have, hitherto, made it a maxim to go to war with France and Spain, whenever they had a fleet. The appearance of a formidable French fleet upon the ocean, has been offence enough to provoke a war. We must now add America; for America, if subdued, would be ever ready to revolt afresh.

"France, he subjoins, expects from the Independence of America, and the acquisition of the West India Islands, the sovereignty of the British seas, if not of Great Britain itself."

France expects only the freedom of the seas, and why should she not expect them? Have we any charter from above, for the government of this ocean? Sovereignty of the seas will never again be permitted to any nation. We have boasted of it, until we have revolted all mankind; America herself will never suffer France to hold the sovereignty of the seas, any more than England. No nation that ever arose upon the globe, had such powerful motives to maintain a perfect freedom of navigation and of commerce among all nations as she has. No nation ever had such advantages and resources to assist the maritime powers to support it. She is as sensible of this as we are. If by our unbridled rage we drive her to the provocation, and the inactivity of the neutral powers should permit it; she may form such further connections with France and Spain, as may give them a superiority of naval power over us, that will be terrible to us. But America herself will never suffer any power of Europe again that decided superiority over all commercial nations, which we have vainly boasted of, and which the past tameness of mankind has permitted. And America, little as she is thought of, will forever have it in her power, by joining with a majority of maritime powers, to preserve their Freedom. The only possible means then of preventing France from obtaining and preserving for some time a superiority over us at sea, is to make peace, and regain not the domination, but the neutrality of America, and our share of her commerce. Thus, and thus only, we may save the West India islands, and an equal freedom of the seas. By making peace at present, we may have more in American trade in future than France, and derive more support to our navy than she will to her marine. But by pushing the war, we weaken ourselves, and strengthen France and Spain every day, to such a degree, that in the end they may acquire such a superiority as will endanger our liberty.[4]

But if Great Britain is to lose the West-India islands, and the sovereignty of the seas, by the Independence of America, who is to gain them? If France is to gain them, are they not as valuable objects to her as to England? Are not their riches as glittering in the eyes of the French as the English? Are they not then as urgent a motive to them to continue the war as to us? We come again once more to the old question, who is likely to hold out longest? The immense resources of France, Spain and America, or the exhausted kingdom of Great Britain?

---

[4] For this sentence, see ibid., p. 790.

LETTER IV

Parker's General Advertiser and Morning Intelligencer
September 3, 1782

SIR,   *Paris, January 30, 1782.*
The writer on the consequences of American independency proceeds, "It has been asserted, that America will be led, from motives
of interest, to give the preference in trade to this country, because
we can supply her with manufactures cheaper than she can raise
them, or purchase them from others." He has not favoured us
with his opinion, whether we can supply them cheaper than others.
If we can, the consequence is certain, that though independent,
they will trade with us, in preference to others. If we cannot, they
will trade with others, in preference to us, though they should again
become dependent. They now know the world, and they will
make use of it, and the world will make use of them. Dependent,
or independent, it will make very little difference. It is not doubted,
at present, that we can sell our commodities to them cheaper, and
give them a better price for theirs than other nations. But how long
will this last? Certainly not long, if the war continues.

That we, or any other nation in Europe, can supply her with
manufactures cheaper than she can raise them, in time of peace,
is most certain. Europe has a warrantee upon America for this for
centuries to come, in the immense regions of uncultivated lands. It
is demonstrably certain, that so long as wild land is to be had
cheap, and it will be for centuries so long, America will continue
to exchange the productions of her agriculture for the manufactures
of Europe. So long the manufacturers, who may emigrate from
Europe, will soon be metamorphosed into farmers, because they
will find, as they always have found, that they can advance themselves and their children the faster by it.

It is very true, "that she possesses, and can produce a greater variety of raw materials, than any other country on the globe," but it by no means follows that it will be her interest to manufacture them, because a day's labour, worth two shillings, in a manufacture, produces but two shillings, whereas a day's labour, on wild land, produces the two shillings in immediate production, and makes that land itself worth two shillings more. We may, therefore, absolutely depend, that at a peace, America will have her manufactures from Europe, and, if it is not our fault, from us.

But, continues the writer, "a commercial alliance is already ratified, greatly injurious to the trade of Great Britain." The commercial alliance with France engages a free trade between those two nations. We may make a commercial alliance with America, and engage a free trade with her too. There is no article in the treaty with France which gives her any exclusive privilege in trade, or that excludes Great Britain from any branch of American trade. It is at this moment as open and free to us, as any other nation, and it is our imprudence that we are throwing it away. Do we suppose that France will give up the benefit she has obtained by this treaty? Is not the commerce, the navy, the independence, and existence of France as a maritime power, at stake? Does it not depend upon American independence? If it does not, it will depend upon her rendering the Colonies, after a mock submission, useless to us, by fomenting continual broils and wars between us and them, and upon getting that commerce clandestinely, that by the treaty she may have openly. Will she not contend as earnestly for her independence and existence as we do for a chimera? The commercial treaty with France is no otherwise injurious to the trade of Great Britain, than as it is a breach of our monopoly, which is broke in an hundred ways, and never to be repaired, if this treaty is annulled.

"Should France succeed in supporting American independence, no one can doubt that other treaties, still more injurious, will be added." Does he mean that America will make treaties of commerce with other maritime nations? This she will do, but upon the same footing of equality, freedom and reciprocity; without excluding us, unless we drive her to despair and revenge, and the same passions that we now indulge against her. Make peace now, and you are safe against all unequal treaties. Other nations must have an equal right to American trade with France and us. The maritime powers all see it, and we may depend upon it, they will take care to secure themselves both against us and France. "When America shall have a separate and distinct interest of her own to pursue, her views will be enlarged, her policy will become exerted to her own benefit."

Does this writer suppose the Americans so ignorant and stupid as not to know this, as well as he? Does he coolly think that they wish to have their views contracted, and their policy exerted against her own benefit, as it used to be, or to the benefit of others, exclusive of her own. It must be an icy soul indeed that can wish itself smaller, or that can desire to have its understanding employed against itself. Is this an argument to prove that the far greater part of the people wish to return to our Government? This could be narrowing their views indeed; but this writer may be assured that this evil, if it be one to us, is already done; their views are already enlarged, they know one another; they know us; and they know the rest of Europe better than ever they did. They know what they are capable of, and what Europe wants.

"Her interest, instead of being united with, will become not only different from, but opposite to that of Great Britain." While we continue her enemy, it is her interest to weaken us as much as she can. But nothing can be clearer, than that her interest will not be opposite to that of any power in Europe, that will trade with her. She will grow; and every power in Europe that trades with her, will grow too in consequence of that trade, and ours more than any other.

"She will perceive that manufactures are the greatest foundation of Commerce." The productions of agriculture are a foundation of commerce, as well as manufactures are.

"That commerce is the great means of acquiring wealth." But manufactures are not the foundations of her commerce, nor is commerce her great means of acquiring wealth. Agriculture, and the continued augmentation of the value of land by improvement, are the great source of her wealth: and agriculture and commerce are but secondary objects, which do not bear a proportion to the former of one to twenty. It is her interest to attend to manufactures for filling up interstices of time, and no farther: and to commerce, to send her superfluous productions abroad, and bring back what she wants, and to be carriers, for the sake of selling her ships and commodities; but all her commerce and manufactures center and terminate in the improvement of land, and will infallibly continue to do so, as long as there shall remain wild land in America: so that it is politically impossible, that she should ever interfere with Europe, either in manufactures or commerce, for centuries to come. In the nature of things she can carry on no manufactures and no commerce which will not be useful to Europe, instead of interfering with it, and to us more than any other, if we would cease our absurd hostilities.

"Bounties will be granted to encourage manufactures, and duties laid to disencourage or prohibit foreign importations!" Will the farmers vote away their money to encourage manufactures, when they can import them cheaper? Will merchants give theirs to strip themselves of the profit of importing? And where is the manufacturing interest to vote at all? All this is against reason and universal experience; a clearer demonstration of this cannot be given than in the instances of salt petre and salt.

Bounties have been given this war upon these articles, manufactured in America, because we would not suffer them to import them. And such is the ingenuity and invention of these people, that hundreds of tons of salt petre were produced in a few months, and the women learned to make it in their families, as they make soap. Salt works were erected upon the sea coast of the whole Continent and they are now able to supply themselves with these articles when they can't get them from Europe but it is at the expense of the interest of agriculture, and when their trade began to open again, these manufactures declined; and they now revive and decline, like ebb and tide, as there happens to be scarcity or plenty imported —and thus it must be.

LETTER V

Parker's General Advertiser and Morning Intelligencer
September 11, 1782

SIR,   *Paris, February 1, 1782.*
"An uniformity of laws and religion, united with a subordination to the same supreme authority, forms the national attachment; but when the laws and supreme authority are abolished, the manners, habits, and customs derived from them, will soon be effaced. The Americans have already instituted governments opposite to the prin-

ciples upon which the British government is established. New laws are made in support of their new political systems, and of course destructive of the national attachment. The new States, altogether popular, their laws resemble those of the democratical cantons of Switzerland, not those of Great Britain. Thus we find, in their first act, the strongest of all proofs, of an aversion in their rulers to our national policy, and a sure foundation laid to obliterate all affections and attachment to this country among the people. The attachment, then arising from a similarity of laws, habits, and manners, will last not longer than between the United Provinces and Spain, or the Corsicans and Genoese, which was changed, from the moment of their separation, into an enmity that is not worn out to this day."

How is it possible for those rulers, in a government altogether popular, who are the creatures of the people, and constantly dependent upon them for their political existence, to have the strongest aversion to the national policy of Great Britain; and at the same time, for the far greater part of the people, to wish and hope for an Union with that country, and to be ready to unite in reducing the power of those rulers, as this writer asserts, I know not. I leave him to reconcile it. But his consistency, and his sincerity, are points of no consequence to the Public.[5]

It is very true that there is no strong attachment in the minds of the Americans to the laws and government of Great Britain. The contrary is true; they have almost universally a strong aversion to those laws and that government. There is a deep and forcible antipathy to two essential branches of the British Constitution, the monarchichal and the aristocratical. There is no country upon earth where the maxims, that all power ought to reside in the great body of the people, and all honours and authorities to be frequently derived from them, are so universally and sincerely believed as in America. All hereditary titles, powers, and dignities, are detested from one end of the Continent to the other; and nothing contributed more to unite all America in the late resistance, than the attempt, by an Act of Parliament, to render one branch of the legislature in the council of the Massachuset's, independent of the people and their representatives. The government of these Colonies have all been popular from their first establishment. It was wise,

---

[5] For this paragraph, see Adams to the president of Congress, June 17, 1780, ibid., p. 796.

just, politic, and necessary, that they should be so. Nothing but
that importance that was given by these governments to the common
people, even to artisans and labouring men, and that comfortable
state of life which is the fruit of it, could ever have peopled
America. The severe labours of the field, in a wild country, and
the dangers of the wilderness, where Planters were forced to carry
thir arms and their instruments of husbandry together to raise
their bread, would have totally discouraged these settlements, if
life had not been sweetened by superior liberty for themselves, and
the prospect of it for their children. The first Planters of New
England, Winthcap, Winslow, Saltenstall, Cotton, Wilson, Norton,
and many others, were great men: they modelled their governments
professedly upon the plan of the ancient Republicks of Greece.
Penn, who founded the colony which bears his name, was another,
and his form of government was as popular, as any in New England.
Sir Walter Rawleigh did nearly the same in Virginia; so that democratical sentiments and principles were not confined to one Colony,
or one part of the Continent, but they run through it. Even in
New York and Virginia and New Hampshire, &c. where the councils were appointed by the crown, these very counsellors were seized
with a strong proportion of the spirit of the people, and were
obliged always to give way to the popular torrent. It is no wonder
then, that every State upon the Continent has instituted a democ-
racy, and that the people are universally fond of their new government. And a philosopher, who considers their situation, planted in
a new country, with immense regions to fill up, by increasing
population and severe labour, will see and acknowledge, that these
kinds of governments are best adapted to their circumstances, but
calculated to promote their happiness, their population, their agriculture, manufactures and commerce, as well as their defence. It is
the interest of all Europe, that they should enjoy these forms of
government. They are best adapted to preserve peace, for the
people always sigh for peace, and detest war; and it is their interest
as well as inclination. It is the interest, and ought to be the inclination of every nation in Europe to let them enjoy it. As to the
affection and attachment to this country, there was always more
noise made about it than sense in it. The affection of one nation
for another, at 3,000 miles distance, is never a strong passion. The
Americans love and adore their country; but America is their
country, not this Island. There are few connections by blood
between that country and this, but what are worn out of memory

by age. Why, then, should we amuse ourselves with unnatural
expectations? We shall never have any hold on the love of America,
but what we obtain, by making it their interest to be our friends, in
a fair and equal commerce, and by favouring their benevolent views
of planting freedom, toleration, humanity, and policy, in the new
world, for the happiness of the human species in both worlds. They
are a people whose feelings are too refined, whose views are too
enlarged for us, sunk as we are in dissipation, avarice, and pleasure.
They think the cause of their country a sacred truth deposited in
their hands by Providence for the happiness of millions yet unborn.
They now think their liberty can never be safe under government
of any European nation, the idea of coming again under which
strikes them with horror. The frozen souls of this country may
scribble, speculate, and fight as they please, they never will have
any future advantage from that, but in the way of a fair and equal
commerce with them as independent states.

This author is certainly just in his sentiments, that the attachment
to England from a similarity of religion, is also very feeble. There
is no predominant religion, and it is their policy that there never
shall be. They are of all the religious societies in Europe; they
are Churchmen, Lutherans, Calvinists, Methodists, Presbyterians,
Moravians, Congregationalists, Quakers, Anabaptists, Menonists,
Swinfielders, Dumplers, and Roman Catholicks.

If the attachments arising from laws and government, from religion, customs, habits, fashions, and language, are such feeble ties,
as this writer very justly represents them, what authority can we
ever have over them, but by their general interests in a fair and
equal commerce, as independent states? Will this writer say, it is
their interest to become again dependent upon us? He has many
times admitted, in effect, in this very pamphlet, that it is not. An
American, even a Tory in America, will readily admit, they ever
have admitted that Independence would be the most prosperous
and glorious event for America, if she could obtain it. They
never contended for any thing, but the American inability to preserve it against the power of Great Britain. What would the rest
of Europe say, if we were gravely to tell them, that it is the interest
of America to come again under our dominion and monopoly?
The interest in America in her independence is too clear a point
to be contested. How then are we to govern them? Are we to govern
and monopolize them, against their interest and inclination, by
force? With all their power and resources, and the aids of France

and Spain, and Holland, favoured, encouraged and abetted by all
the maritime powers of Europe? We have really a task beyond our
forces. Surely, in such a situation, peace with America, and a
treaty of commerce upon terms of perfect equality and reciprocity
would be safe, an honourable, and an advantageous peace.

LETTER VI

Parker's General Advertiser and Morning Intelligencer
September 27, 1782

Paris, February 2, 1782.
If "we receive from the West India Islands certain commodities necessary to manufactures," as the cool reasoner on the consequences of
American Independence pretends, "which we can procure from no
other country;" is not this a motive for France to continue the
war, as forcible as for *us?* The rivalry, and the enmity, between
England and France, is so ancient, and so deeply rooted in the
hearts of the two nations, that each considers the weakening of
the other as a gain to itself. The English have, a long time, made
it a maxim never to suffer France either to have a navy, or a
flourishing commerce. An active, prosperous trade, or a formidable
marine, have ever been considered as a legitimate cause of war.
And whether we think of it coolly or not, England would have been
at war with France before now, if we had never had any war with
America, merely to burn, sink, and destroy her Marine. Can we
be so ignorant of the human heart then, as not to know that
depriving us of these commodities, which we derive from the West
India Islands, and which are necessary to our manufactures, will
be an inducement to our enemies to continue the war? Depriving
us of a commodity, taking from us a manufacture, is motive enough,
if our enemies act upon the same maxims that we do; but, adding
the commodity or the manufacture to themselves, is a double
motive. In short, is it possible for this writer to adduce one

reason to us to continue the war, which is not also a cool argument for France, Spain, and America to continue it? The question still is, Which can hold out longest, France, who has yet laid on one new imposition, or we, who add annually almost a million to our perpetual taxes? America, whose whole national debt does not amount to more than five million, or we, whose debt is more than 200 millions, at least fifty of which have already been added by this war? *By making peace, we have the Islands, with their commodities; by continuing the war, we lose them infallibly.*

"But this is not all," says this cool disclaimer: "We must add to our loss of seamen, sustained by the Independence of America, at least twenty thousand more, who have been bred and maintained in the trade from Great Britain to the West Indies, and in the West Indies trade among themselves, and with other parts, amounting in the whole to upwards of eighty thousand; a loss which cannot fail to affect the sensibility of every man who loves this country, and knows that its safety can only be secured by its Navy."

But has it been considered, that neither of the powers at war have any pretence of claim to these Islands now? That they will have pretences upon them if they take them, which we cannot hinder if we continue the war? *That once taken by France, America is bound by treaty to warrant them to her?* This treaty lasts no longer than this war. Another war, America will be under no such obligations, unless, by continuing the war, we should compel her into further treaties, which *may be*, though she would be adverse to them. Is it prudency in us to hazard so much upon the events of war, which are always uncertain, where forces are equal? But we are now most impolitically entangling ourselves in a war where the forces and resources are two to one against us? But will France and Spain be the less zealous to conquer the English Islands, because, by this means, they shall certainly take away so many seamen, and share them with America? Annexing [6] these Islands to France and Spain, will increase the trade of France, Spain, Denmark, the United Provinces, of the Low Countries, and the United States of America, and the twenty thousand seamen will be divided in some proportion between all these powers. The Dutch and the Americans will have the carriage of a great part of this trade, in consequence of the dismemberment of these Islands from you, and annexation to

---

[6] For this and the next sentence, see Adams to the president of Congress, June 16, 1780, ibid., p. 791.

France and Spain. Do we expect to have these things by continuing
the war? If we do, I wish we could reflect *more coolly* upon things.
Every success we have yet had, in the whole course of this war, has
been owing to fortunate contingencies, or the mistaken policy of
our enemies. It is too much for us to presume, that a series of
miracles will be wrought for our deliverance, or that our enemies
will never discover where their strength lies. We may bless our stars,
and not our wisdom, that we have now an army, a navy, or an island
in the West Indies.

"Will not Great Britain lose much of her Independence, if obliged
to other countries for her naval stores?" Has she lost her Independence? Has she not been obliged to other countries for naval stores
these five years?

"In the time of Queen Anne, we paid 3l. a barrel for tar to the
extortionate Swede; and such was the small demand of those countries for the manufactures of this, that the ballance of trade was
greatly in their favour. The gold we obtained in other commerce,
was continually pouring into their laps. But we have reduced that
ballance, by our importation of large quantities of those supplies
from America."

But what is to hinder Great Britain from importing these large
quantities of pitch, tar, and turpentine, from America, after we shall
be wise enough to acknowledge and guarantee her Independence, by
an honourable and advantageous peace with her? Great Britain may
be obliged to give a price somewhat higher, because other nations
will import them too. But this augmentation of price will probably
be very little. Will the prospect of this higher price induce America
to give up her Independence, and her new Governments, which,
whatever we may think, are more firmly and solidly established than
ours is? Will not our manufacturers purchase pitch from independent America? Will the prospect which is opened to the other maritime powers, of drawing these supplies, as well as those of masts,
yards, bowsprits, ship timber, and ready-wrought ships too, make
them less zealous to support American Independence? Will the
increase of the demand upon the Northern Powers for those Articles,
in consequence of the destruction of the British monopoly, in
America, make these powers less inclined to American Independency? The British monopoly and bounties, in fact, reduced the price
of these articles in the Northern markets. The ceasing of that
monopoly, and those bounties, will rather raise the price in the
Baltic: Because those States in America, where pitch and tar chiefly

grow, have so many articles of more profitable cultivation, that, without bounties, it is not likely that trade will flourish to a degree, to reduce the prices in the North of Europe.[7]

Every day shews us more and more, that we undertook this war too rashly; *without considering ourselves*; without knowing the character and resources of America, and without weighing the relations between America and Europe. ——— [material missing] they have all decided this question against us, and in favour of America, as fully as even France has done. They all think that the cause of America is just, and that every one of them is interested in supporting her Independence. They have not had motives so pressing as France, Spain, and Holland, to engage in open war; but the measures they are taking, are as clearly in favour of America. There is not a power upon earth so much interested as America in the capital point which they are establishing, That free ships make free goods.

"Should a war take place between us and the Northern Powers, where are we to procure our naval stores?" I answer, make peace with America, and procure them from her. But when you go to war with America and the Northern Powers at once, you will get them no where. This writer appears to have had no suspicion, when he wrote his book, of the real intentions of the Northern Powers.[8] What he thinks now, after their confederation against Great Britain, I know not. It is remarkable that this confederation was known in Europe eighteen months, and in the American Congress twelve months (not indeed as an act executed, but as a sentiment and design in which they were all agreed, and for which they were all making preparations) before it was either known or attended to by that Administration, of which Lord North was the ostensible Premier. We may affect to be as much astonished as we will. We may cry: "How sharper than a serpent's tooth it is to have thirteen *thankless* children!" *We may growl amidst the tempest*, like Lear, and cry to the thunders: "Rumble your fill! Fight whirlwind! hail! and fire!" But we must submit to fate. Her ordinances cannot be repealed by our Parliament, which has not yet claimed jurisdiction over her in all cases whatsoever.

---

[7] For this paragraph, see ibid., p. 791.
[8] For this sentence, see ibid., p. 792.

LETTER VII

Parker's General Advertiser and Morning Intelligencer
October 2, 1782

Paris, February 3d, 1782

The writer, on the consequences of American Independence says that "France has long struggled to rival us in our manufactures in vain; this (i.e., American Independence) will enable her to do it with effect."

If England would awake out of her dream, and make peace, acknowledge American Independence, and acknowledge the American treaties with France, and make a similar treaty of commerce with the United States, upon the most generous principles of equality and reciprocity, neither France nor any other nation of Europe would be able to rival England in those manufactures which we most wanted in America, those of wool and iron: The English manufactures, in these articles are at present so much better, and the Americans are so much more accustomed to them, that this trade would return to its old channel, and the American demand for them, and for many other articles of our manufactures would increase in proportion, as the population increases in America, and as their commerce with each other and with other nations increases, and the consequent means of paying England for what they purchase. This nation would find themselves so far from being materially hurt, by American Independence, that they would see a prosperity introduced here in consequence of it, that would excite the utmost astonishment at our own obstinacy, in contending so long, at the expense of so much blood and treasure, against it, provided we are wise enough to lay aside our groundless jealousies, and that hostile disposition towards America which is once more indulged with so much rancour; and provided we take care at the peace to settle all questions about boundaries, so as to prevent our own people from encroaching upon them; and provided we do not meanly aim at excluding them from any branches of commerce, fisheries or naval powers which God and nature have destined to them. If we will indulge the base passions of envy, jealousy and hatred against them, we may depend upon a dreadful enemy in them: but if we had magnanimity enough to comply with what appears to be the settled digested system of all the other maritime powers of Europe relative to America, to treat them with candour and friendship, we shall find as much real advantage from them, and more too, than we ever did. All will depend upon ourselves. Nothing is wanting but common sense.

But if we pursue this war, destroying the lives, and distressing the commerce of America, we shall feel from that country such states of deadly hate, as will finally ruin our credit, destroy our manufactures, reduce to nothing our influence in Europe, depress our naval power to such an inferiority to France and Spain, as we never shall recover; leave the East Indies and Ireland in a state of Independency too, and the West India Islands ready to petition any other power for protection, and indeed this island itself at the mercy of an invader. If we continue this war, France and Spain too will be able to rival us in manufactures. They are both attentive at this time to this object; they are not only endeavouring to introduce our manufactures, but to accommodate them more to the taste and use of the Americans. And the Americans are daily growing more familiar with French articles, and acquiring a taste for them. The advantages in trade, already granted to Ireland, and the consequent growth of manufactures there, will infinitely facilitate the introduction and improvement of manufactures; and the emigration of manufactures into France and Spain, by means of the intimate intercourse between Ireland and those kingdoms. In short, the continuance of the war will indeed be fatal: it will enable France to rival us in effect in our most essential interests; and there has hardly ever happened among mankind so obstinate and so blind a perseverance in error so obvious, for so long a time, as we have already pursued this ruinous war. Let us open our eyes. We are amused with insinuations that France is sick with the part she has acted. This is to suppose her sick of the wisest, most successful, most honourable, and noble part she ever acted. Think as we will, all the rest of Europe and America are convinced of this: and if we had sold ourselves to France, we could not serve her more essentially, in every interest, commercial, naval, political, or economical, than by continuing this war.

Our cool thinker goes on, "We receive, say he, from the West India Islands, certain commodities, absolutely necessary to carry on our manufactures to any advantage and extent, which we can procure from no other country. We must take the remains from France or America, after they have supplied themselves, and fulfilled their contracts with their allies at their own prices, and loaded with the expense of foreign transportation, if we are permitted to trade for them at all." If this was intended as an argument for continuing the war, I should have thought it the raving of the delirium of a fever, rather than a cool thought. Is it possible to urge an argument more clear for making peace now, while we may have our islands? How are we to supply our islands with lumber, and other necessaries, if we continue the war? A man who has really thought coolly upon the subject, wou'd have advised us to make peace and save our West India islands. He would have told us, that by continuing the war, we should certainly lose them, and with them the articles so necessary to our manufactures. America does not wish the English Islands in the hands of the French. She is very ready to warrantee to the English all that are not taken, and very probably France would restore those that are, in exchange for other possessions which we have taken from them. America cannot wish to continue the war, because she gains nothing,* except in military skill; in the advancement of agriculture and manufactures, laying the strongest possible foundation for future commerce, prosperity and naval power. France and Spain indeed may be supposed to wish its continuance, because they are gaining every year conquest of territory, as well as augmentation of manufactures and commerce, naval power, and political consideration in Europe. THE ENGLISH MALADY IS UPON US. THE DISPOSITION TO SUICIDE, WHICH DESTROYS SO MANY INDIVIDUALS AMONG US, HAS SEISED THE PUBLIC; WHEN PEACE LEADS TO GLORY, AND WAR TO NOTHING BUT DISGRACE AND RUIN, WE FALL HEADLONG INTO THE ABYSS OF THE ONE, AND LEAVE THE PLEASANT AND SAFE PATH OF THE OTHER.

* Nothing except these! Yes! and much more than what the letter writer has enumerated. She gains a glorious triumph over tyranny and ambition; a reparation, purchased gallantly with the best blood of her fellow citizens, for the violated rights of man; the power of establishing peace, freedom, virtue, and independency, upon the spot, which was intended for the scene of their extinction; and of leaving an aweful and instructive lesson to the nations of the earth, for ever.

LETTER VIII

Parker's General Advertiser and Morning Intelligencer
October 17, 1782

Paris, February 4th, 1782

The Cool Thoughts go on. "Timber of every kind, iron, salt-petre, tar, pitch, turpentine, and hemp, are raised, and manufactured in America. Fields of an hundred thousand acres of hemp are to be seen spontaneously growing between the Ohio and Mississippi, and of a quality little inferior to the Europeans."

And is not this enough to cool the English courage, in the pursuit of a chimera? Is it possible to keep one country that has an abundance of these articles, and skill to use them, dependent on another? It is a maxim among the sons of Neptune, that "with wood, iron, and hemp, mankind may do what they please." America not only has them in plenty, but artists and seamen to employ them, fifteen hundred miles of sea coast, and a hundred excellent harbours to use them in, at three thousand miles distance from her enemy, who is surrounded with nations that are courting her friendship. Are not these articles as precious to France, Spain, and Holland, as to England? Will not these powers be proportionably active to procure a share of them, or a liberty to trade in them, as England will be to defend her monopoly of them? And will not America be as alert to obtain the freedom of selling them to the best advantage in a variety of markets, as other nations will for that of purchasing them?

This writer is so cool, that he thinks of nothing. A little warmth of imagination would be of use to him; it would present to his view a variety of considerations that have never occured to him. Three millions of people in America, and all the nations of Europe, have as great a right to the common blessings of Providence, as the inhabitants of this island, some of whom wish to lord it over all. The Americans have as good a claim to the use of the earth, air, and seas, as the Britons. What right has Briton to shut them up in the prison of a monopoly, and prevent them from giving and receiving happiness from the rest of mankind? Did the Creator make that quarter of the globe for the use of this Island exclusively? This may be a cool thought, but a very narrow one. There is another very serious consideration, that our coolness, or our heat, makes us incapable of attending to. Great Britain, separated from America, has, in the course of this war, displayed a power and resources, vastly greater, especially at sea, than the other maritime powers ever before believed she possessed. America, separated from Great Britain, has displayed a power and resources ten times greater than any power in Europe, (even Great Britain herself,) ever suspected her to have. These are two discoveries that the other maritime powers have made. They now see, to a demonstration, that if Great Britain and America should ever be again united under one domination, there would be an end of the liberty of all other nations upon the seas. All the commerce and navigation of the world would be swallowed up in one frightful despotism, in this Island. The Princes of Europe, therefore, are now unanimously determined that America shall never again come under the British government. Even if the Americans themselves desired it, which it is most certain they do not, nor ever will, the powers of Europe would not suffer it. For what object then are the English shedding their blood, and spending their millions?

"Will the Coasting trade, that of the Baltic and Mediterranean, with the small intercourse the English have with other nations in our own bottoms, furnish seamen for a Navy, necessary for the protection of Great Britain and its trade?"

According to this supposition, Great Britain will have no other trade, than that of the Coast, the Mediterranean, and the Baltic to protect, and she may protect her trade in that case as well as Portugal and Holland, &c. protect theirs, and in the same manner. And to this situation she will certainly come, if she continues the war for any length of time. If the American Congress should take the resolution of prohibiting the importation of British manufactures, directly, or indirectly, from any part of the world, a part which they will likely to take, in order to weaken Great Britain, and strengthen their allies; if she continues this war, she will perceive the sources of her trade drying away, and the waters gliding into other channels; her seamen lessening and consuming, those of her enemies increasing; her capacity to defend her Islands, and even her East India trade, every day lessening, and that of her enemies to invade them every day increasing. So that it must end in the very evil this writer suggests: Whereas, if Great Britain makes peace now, the evil is avoided.

"Will her mariners continue as they are, when her manufactures are labouring under the disadvantage of receiving their materials at higher and exorbitant prices, and selling at foreign markets at a certain loss?"

I suppose the English will be able to purchase of the Americans their materials as cheap as other nations. But do they expect ever to recover her monopoly so as to prevent other nations from getting American materials? So as to prevent the Americans from getting manufactures, productions, and all sorts of merchandizes from other nations? Let us consider this cooly. How much trouble did it cost them to prevent this communication before the war, when the American mind was possessed with all that fear, which is essentially the characteristic of monopolized colonies? When the American merchants had never traveled but to England: When their masters of vessells and seamen were ignorant of the French coast, and were taught to dread it as unknown and dangerous: Were the English ever able, under all these advantages, to prevent the Americans from eluding our act of navigation? But what has happened since this war broke out? Young American merchants, from every one of the Thirteen States, have crouded to France, and other parts of Europe, in great numbers, have studied the wants of France, and the articles she has which America wants, and the prices of all are stated in journals and memorandum books, which we can never obliterate. When such numbers of American masters of vessells have now explored the whole coast of France, so as to conduct vessels, wherever they please, even without pilots: When young Physicians, and Divines, and Lawyers, have travelled to France, formed acquaintance with men of letters, and established correspondences, which never can be extinquished: When American merchants and mariners have explored the creeks, inlets, and harbours of North America itself, ten times more perfectly than they were ever known before, to elude our frigates and cruisers: After all this, can we cooly suppose that the English ever will regain our monopoly, and prevent smuggling? If the English were to conquer America; if she was to submit, (suppositions as wild as can well be made,) no Custom-house officer, of any candour, will give it as his opinion, that they ever should be able to execute the act of navigation again in America. Fifty thousand regular soldiers, posted on the sea coast, and fifty men of war constantly cruising, an expense that would be greater than the monopoly ever was worth, would not effect it. Be not deceived! Impossibilities cannot be performed by Great Britain, and if her monopoly be gone, what is she contending for? The seamen then, which were secured to her by the monopoly, are gone for ever; and her only policy is to be as generous and magnanimous as France: in this way she has it in her power to prevent America from getting any destructive advantage of her but by continuing the war, she will infallibly compleat the triumph of America and her own humiliation—for civil, political, military, literary, commercial, and naval connections between America in every part of it, and France, and Spain, and Holland, are multiplying every day, and never will be checked but by a peace.

But what is the tendency of this argument, about the loss of seamen? If it serves to convince Britain that she should continue the war, does it not convince the allies that they ought to continue it too? They are to get all that England is to lose; and America is to be the greatest gainer of all. Whereas, she is not only to lose these objects, but her liberty too, and the lives of her best men, in infamy, if she is subdued: France, Spain, and Holland, and all the other Maritime Powers, are to gain a share of the objects, if Britain loses them. Whereas they not only lose all share in them, but even the safety and existence of their flag upon the ocean may be lost, if American is reduced, and the British monopoly of American Trade, Fisheries, and Seamen revived.

But let us coolly consider a few of the consequences of the redoubtable English conquests of America! Multitudes of the most learned, ingenious, and at present reputable men in the Thirteen United States, must fly abroad. Some of them the English would arrest; some of them would not fly to save their lives, but would remain there, to exhibit to mankind spectacles that Sydney and Russell never exceeded; but multitudes would fly. What would be the policy of France and Spain? Would they not immediately form American Brigades, as they have done Irish Brigades? Would not these be asylums for American Officers and Soldiers? Would not these hold constant correspondence and commerce too with America, and keep America on tiptoe for fresh revolts? Would it not cost America the constant maintenance of a larger fleet and army, than have been employed in the conquest, to preserve it?

The English are pursuing the most absurd war, that ever was raised by rational beings. Their very successes are ruinous to them, and useful to America. If they take a city, they only establish dis-affection, open a trade which supplies the Americans with every thing they want, and their soldiers teach the citizens, and even the children, every branch of the art of war, the discipline manoeuvres of troops, cavalry, artillery, &c. If their men of war and privateers take American ships, it only serves to form American naval officers and seamen, who are made prisoners, to as perfect a mastery of every branch of the sea service as their own. If American privateers take British seamen, they find beef and pudding, and grog and beer, among American sailors, and enlist with the utmost chearfulness into their service.

Let the British go on, and compleat the glorious work of destruc-tion to themselves, and glory to America and the rest of mankind. Such infatuation is in the order of Providence. Our *Thinker* ought to excuse me, if I am as much too warm as he is too cool.

LETTER IX

Parker's General Advertiser and Morning Intelligencer
October 23, 1782

Paris, February 5th, 1782.

The American Refugees, in England, are so great an obstacle in the way of peace, that it seems not improper for me to take notice of them. The first and greatest of them, the late Mr. Hutchinson, is no more. He was born to be the cause, the object, and the victim of popular rage; and he died a day after the commencement of the insurrections in London, and just soon enough to escape the sight of the vengeance against Lord Mansfield's house, which so exactly resembled that which was fifteen years ago inflicted on his own. Descended [9] from an ancient and honourable American family; born

[9] The remainder of this and the three following paragraphs are incorporated from Adams to the president of Congress, June 17, 1780, ibid., pp. 794–96. For the publication in America of Adams's sketch of Hutchinson, see Bernard Bailyn, *The Ordeal of Thomas Hutchinson* (Cambridge: Harvard University Press, 1974), pp. 375–76.

and educated in that country; professing all the zeal of the congregational religion; affecting to honour the character of the first planters; early initiated into public business; industrious and indefatigable in it; beloved and esteemed by the people; elected and entrusted by them, and their Representatives; his views opened and extended by repeated travels in Europe; minutely informed in the history of his country; author of an history of it, which was extensively read in Europe; engaged in much correspondence, in Europe, as well as America; favoured by the Crown of Great Britain, and possessed of its honours and emoluments; in these circumstances, and with these advantages, he was perhaps the only man, in the world, who could have brought on the controversy, between Great Britain and America, at the time, and in the manner, in which it was begun, and involved the two countries in an enmity, which must end in their everlasting separation. This was his character; and these his memorable actions. An inextinguishable ambition, which was ever discerned among his other qualities, which grew with his growth, and strengthened with his age and experience, at last predominated over ever other passion of his heart and principle of his mind: rendered him credulous of every thing which favoured his ruling passion, but blind and deaf to every thing that opposed it: to such a degree, that his representations, with those of his friend and instrument, Bernard, drew on the King, Ministry, Parliament and Nation to concert those measures, which must end in a reduction of the power of the English, if they do not change their conduct, but in the exaltation and glory of America.

There are visible traces of his councils in a number of pamphlets not long since published in England, and ascribed to Mr. Galloway. It is most probable, they were concerted between Administration and the Americans in general here, and Mr. Galloway was given out as the ostensible, as he probably was the principal author.

The "Cool Thoughts on the Consequences of American Independence," although calculated to inflame a warlike nation, are sober reasons for America to defend her Independence and her alliance.

The pamphlet says "It has often been asserted that Great Britain has expended, in settling and defending America, more than she will ever be able to repay, and that it will be more to the profit of this kingdom to give her Independence, and to lose what we have expended, than to retain her a part of its dominions." To this he answers very justly, "that the bounties on articles of commerce, and the expense of the last war, ought not to be charged to America; that the charge of colonial Governments, have been confined to New York, the Carolinas, Georgia, Nova Scotia, and East and West Florida. That New England, New Jersey, Pennsylvania, Delaware and Virginia, have not cost Great Britain a farthing; that the whole expense of the former, is no more than one million seven hundred thousand pounds; and that when we deduct the seven hundred thousand pounds, extravagantly expended in building a key at Hallifax, we can only call it one million."

But the true answer is, that America has already repaid to England an hundred fold for all that has been expended upon her. The profit of her commerce, for one year, has been more than all that this kingdom has expended upon her in one hundred and fifty years. Whence is all the pride of Great Britain? Whence her opulence? Whence her populous cities? Whence multitudes of her cloud-capt towers, her gorgeous palaces and solemn temples, but from the profits of American commerce? But all this would not content her; she must tax America, and rob her of her liberty, as well as monopolize her commerce. The latter she endured, but the former she would not bear, and who can blame her? None, none but those who are conscious of the guilt of forging shackles for her.

This commerce Great Britain might still enjoy, but will not. Why? Because she cannot enjoy it all. Where will be the injury to her from other nations enjoying with her a small share of the blessings of Heaven? If France alone were to possess a share, Great Britain might have some color for jealousy, that she would become dangerous to her; but when America herself in the treaty she sent to France, with a foresight, a refined and enlarged policy that does honour to human nature, so studiously and anxiously guard against excluding any other nation from an equal share in her commerce; when she had coolness and magnanimity enough although under every provocation from Great Britain to resentment, to guard against excluding even her from an equal share of her commerce, what was Great Britain to fear. If she made peace with America, she would not be without friends in Europe; and if her enemies should profit by American commerce she and her friends would profit more. The balance will be preserved, and she will have nothing to fear. Commerce she may have with America, as advantageous as ever, if she does not lose the opportunity: But taxation, domination and monopoly, are gone for ever.

The writer proceeds, "Posterity will feel that America was not only worth all that was spent upon her, but that a just, firm, and constitutional subordination of the Colonies, was absolutely necessary to the independence and existence of Great Britain."

He should have said, That the ancestors of the present English have already found that America was worth all that has been spent upon her; that they have received, and themselves have enjoyed more from her, than all that has been spent; that besides this, they have amased more solid wealth from her, and transmitted down, by inheritance to their children, an hundred fold more than all the cost: *And even now America remains ready to renew her commerce with England to as great an advantage as ever, if they will make a peace.* Are domination and taxation necessary to trade? By no means. Their trade to Portugal and Russia is as profitable, as if these were not independent States.

That a share in the commerce of America is necessary to support long the independence and existence of Great Britain, I readily agree; but this share does not depend upon her having the government of that country, much less upon her drawing taxes from it. This depends upon the wants of America, and the capacity of Great Britain to supply them. Her wants will increase beyond all proportion to the ability of Great Britain to supply in time; and her *Immediate* demand upon her would be greater than she could possibly supply at present, if she made peace.

The independence of America would have no more effect upon the independence of Great Britain, than it either has, or will have, upon that of France or Spain, if she would change our hostile character against America into friendship, [as] they have done. But writers, from private views and private passions, are drawing the English on in error and delusion against their clearest Interest, against the voice of Nature, of Reason, of all Europe, and of GOD!

Letter X

Parker's General Advertiser and Morning Intelligencer
December 26, 1782

Paris, Feb. 6.

Let us proceed with our cool meditations. The author says, "Another argument much relied on by the advocates of American Independence, is, that a similarity of laws, religion, and manners, has formed an attachment between the People of Great Britain and America, which will insure to Great Britain a preference in the trade of America."

A similarity of laws facilitates business. It may be done with more ease, expedition, and pleasure, and with less risque of loss, mistake, or imposition, and consequently with more profit, in a country whose laws are understood, than in another where they are not. A similarity of religion is a motive of preference to those persons who are conscientious, and some such there are among the men of business even of this philosophic age. A similarity of manners and language also prevents many perplexities, delays, and impositions in trade: besides that the pleasures of society and conversation are some motives to a man of business. Laws, religion, manners, and language, therefore, will be motives of preference, *cateris paribus.* After all, however, the goodness and cheapness of commodities will be the only decisive temptations to Americans to come here to market. They can learn languages, enjoy their own religion, among a people of a different one; conform for a time to manners very different to their own, and acquire a knowledge of the laws of the other countries sufficient to do business there, provided they find better and cheaper goods there to be bought, and a better price for those they have to sell. Can the English then give them a better price for their commodities than other nations, and sell them theirs cheaper than others? This is the main question; and there is no doubt that they can, in most articles, at present: it will not be long so. If they give other nations time to establish their manufactures by the continuance of the war, all this may be changed. Do the English expect ever to compel the Americans to take their commodities at a high price, when they can have them abroad at a lower? An American would laugh in your face if you were gravely to tell him so. Can the English trust their Custom House Officers, who are to be appointed in the future, that they would not connive? Did they never hear of merchants privileged to smuggle? Did they never hear of Governors sharing profits? Do they expect the Juries in America will condemn? Do they expect their single Judges of Admiralty will be again admitted in America, to try seizures and questions of civil property at land, where the people have even insisted that Juries should be appointed to try all maritime causes? It is a chimera that the English pursue. If they could re-acquire the Government, they never could execute the laws which guarded the monopoly. They never could execute them before. Now both the knowledge, the temptation, and the facilities to evade and elude them are infinitely multiplied. If they could force a sufficient number of Americans to submit to regain the government, the great body of the people would think them usurpers and tyrants and that they have a right to elude and evade their mandates by every art and every shift. It will be forced government, maintained only by military power, detested and exercrated by the people, even by the most of those who in a fright or a fit of delusion should now submit.

Their acts of trade never were executed in America, excepting only at Boston. At New York, at Philadelphia, at Charles Town, they were constantly evaded. The Custom House Officers never dared to put them in execution. Nay, they were never executed even in Rhode Island and New Hampshire. It was only at Boston, under a military power, and an innumerable host of Custom House Officers, where they were executed at all. And here, at the expense of constant lawsuits, riots, tumults, and thousands of other evils. Before this war, the Americans were almost as ignorant of each other, as they were of Europe. Now they have become acquainted with both. There was little communication or correspondence, and still less trade between one Colony and another since this war. Great numbers of gentlemen of the first characters in the States have met in Congress, where they have learned every thing respecting other States. Officers and armies have marched from one end of the Continent to the other; became intimately acquainted with each other, formed friendships and correspondences with each other that never will cease; became perfectly acquainted with the geography of every province, city, river, creek, plain, and mountain. Waggons and waggoners have constantly passed from Maryland, Pennsylvania, New Jersey, New York, and all New England, to Boston. Do the English suppose they will ever prevent the trade between one colony and another again? Will they prevent tilt hammers from being erected, wool from being waterborne, or tobacco from being sent from Virginia to Boston? An hundred thousand regular soldiers, and every man of war they have in the world, would not accomplish it. But the English are in a dream. They know not what they are contending for. *They think America is in the same situation she was ten years ago.* They either know not, or consider not, what has happened there within these six years. This cool writer himself has been too much warmed with some passion or other to recollect what has passed within his own observation. It is much wished he would give us his *cool Thoughts on the Consequences of American dependence, conquest, and submission.* If he were to reflect upon the subject, he might easily prove, that it would be a constant source of vexation and expence to England, without any profit or advantage. It would be but a momentary, and that an armed, riotous, rebellious and distracted truce; a constant source of fresh American revolts, and fresh foreign wars. The English ought to dread the temporary submission of America, more that America herself. It would be the source of their certain, final ruin; whereas to them it might be only a temporary evil. Every rising country has infinite advantages over a declining one, in every view.

Two Additional, Unpublished Letters
from a Distinguished American

In the Adams Papers, microfilm edition, reel number 351, under the date February 7, 1780, there are two essays, in Adams's best hand-writing, which clearly belong to the Distinguished American series. In a June 1783 letter Jenings informed Adams that all his essays, save "two sheets," had been cut up by the compositors and could not be returned.[10] The "two sheets" Jenings evidently sent back to Adams; they are undoubtedly the February 7 drafts. Adams makes it clear that both drafts were intended refutations to Galloway's *Cool Thoughts*: we are "arrived at the Period long since foreseen and foretold by cooler and deeper Thinkers than this Pamphleteer" (draft one); and "Before We dismiss these cool Thoughts" (draft two). In both drafts, as in the published essays, Adams writes as though he were an Englishman. Finally, there is an editorial addition, in a different hand, on draft one, which clinches the case. The addition is the insertion of the date "Paris—Feb: 7th." [11] Those who assembled the Adams microfilm edition naturally assumed that the inserted date indicated composition on February 7, 1780; what it really shows is that the essay was intended to be the next published in the Distinguished American series, for the last published essay bore the false date "Paris, Feb. 6." The second undated draft bears an editorial correction in the same hand. This draft was written as the conclusion of the series, which amounted, therefore, to twelve essays. The two drafts printed below were composed, it is clear, in July 1780, as were their printed companions. Why Parker did not publish them in his *General Advertiser* is not clear; perhaps the conclusion of peace preliminaries between the United States and Britain made them, in his view, irrelevant.

---

10 Adams Papers microfilm, reel 361.
11 Another note on draft one reads: "See American Bank Gen. Ad. Septr 25."

LETTER XI [12]

To illustrate his argument on the Consequences of American Independence, the Writer subjoins, a Comparison, between the united States and the West Indies. He says the Exports from England were in 1771

	£	S	d
To North America	4,586,882 :	15 :	5
To Dominica	170,623 :	19 :	3
To St. Vincent	36,839 :	10 :	1
To Grenada	123,919 :	4 :	5
Difference	4,255,500 :	1 :	2

"If we reflect on the Extent of Territory, improved and improvable, the Numbers of People, or Mariners, of Shipping, naval Force, raw materials, and Consumption of manufactures, he hopes We should confess the Continent of more Importance than the Islands." He compares them 1. in Point of Extent of Territory. 2. Salubrity of Clymates. 3. Numbers of Inhabitants capable of Waring for the Empire, whereas the Islands are a dead weight in Case of War. 4. Variety of Clymates. If the West Indies furnish Rum, Sugar, Cocoa, Coffee, Paimento and Ginger. The Continent produces Wheat Rye, Barley Oats, Indian Corn, Rice, Flour, Biscuit, Salt Beef, Pork, Venison, Cod, Mackarel, and other Fish and Tobacco. If the West Indies produce some materials for Dyes, as Logwood, Fustick Mahogany and Indigo; the Continent produces Indigo Silk Flax Hemp; Furs and Skins of the Bear, Beaver, otter Muscrat, Deer, Tyger, Leopard, Wildcat, Fox Raccoon; and Pot ash, Pearl ash Copper, and Lead ore, Iron in Pigs and Bars, for our Manufactures; besides all the Articles of naval Stores, Timber, Plank, Boards, Masts, Yards, Ships for Sale, Pitch, Tar, Turpentine, Hemp and Salt Petre. Such

---

[12] This essay is an expansion of Adams's letter to the president of Congress, June 17, 1780 (the second of this date), Adams Papers microfilm, reel 100.

of these Articles as are necessary for the manufactures and Commerce of England were sent there: the surplus only to other Markets, and the proceeds of that surplus remitted in Bills of Exchange or Cash for British manufactures and foreign articles of Commerce."

As to the Consumption of Manufactures, America would demand and consume, if Peace were now made as many and more of our manufactures than she ever did, because her Numbers have greatly increased since this Trade was interrupted. As to our supplying them again with foreign articles of Commerce it is chimerical in Us, to expect it: neither America, nor foreign nations will submit to it. As to the long roll of Articles, which contribute to political, military and naval Power, it is extravagant to hope ever to regain them. All mankind are interested and have the most pressing Motives to Sunder them from Us. They would make Us an universal monarchy.

Power is intoxicating, encroaching and dangerous, in Nations, as well as Individuals. Surrounding nations are jealous, and envyous of a Power that they see growing too formidable for their Safety. Examples are innumerable. Spain under Charles the 5th—France under Louis the 14th were thought by the powers of Europe to have become dangerous, and allmost all the World united to lessen their Power. How did Portugal break off from Spain? How did she maintain her Independency? How does she hold it now? But because that England, France, Holland and other Powers, will not see her again annexed to the Spanish monarchy situated as Portugal is, if she were annexed to Spain it would make her dangerous to the other maritime Powers. How did Holland maintain her Independency? but by the determined aid of England & France? How did the Cantons of Switzerland maintain theirs?

We are arrived at the Period long since foreseen and foretold by cooler and deeper Thinkers than this Pamphleteer. It is an observation of a sage and amiable Writer of the French nation, who has as much respect for England and as little for America as any impartial man in Europe, De Mably, "That the Project of being sole Master of the Sea, and of commanding all the Commerce, is not less chimerical, nor less ruinous than that of Universall Monarchy on Land. And it is to be wished for the Happiness of Europe, that the English may be convinced of this Truth, before they shall have learned it by their own experience. France has already repeated several Times, that it was necessary to establish an Equilibrium, or Ballance of Power, at Sea; and she has not yet convinced any Body because she is the dominant Power, and because they suspect her to desire the abasement of the English, only that she may domineer the more freely, on a Continent. But if England abuses her Power and would exercise a Kind of Tryanny over Commerce, presently all the States that have Vessells and sailors, astonished that they had not before believed France, will join themselves to her to assist her in avenging her Injuries. Principles of Negotiation." n. 90.

The Present Conjunction of Affairs resembles so exactly the Case that is here stated that it seems to be a litteral fulfillment of a Prophesy. A Domination upon the Sea is so much the more dangerous to other commercial and maritime Powers, as it is more difficult to form Alliances and combine Forces at Sea, than at Land, for which Reason it is essential, that the Sovereign of every commercial State, should make his national Flagg be respected, in all the Seas and by all the nations of the World. The English have ever acted upon this Principle, in supporting the Honour of their own, but in late years, inflated with intoxicating dreams of Power, they have grown less and less attentive to it, as it respects the Honour of other Flaggs. Not content with making their Flagg respectable they have grown more and more ambitious of making it terrible. Unwilling to do as they would be done by, and to treat other commercial nations as they insisted upon being treated by them, they have grown continually more and more haughty, turbulent, and insolent upon the seas, and are now never satisfied untill they make all other nations see and feel that they despise them upon that Element. We have not only invaded the universal Liberty of the Americans, by cutting up by the Roots their ancient forms of Government and endeavouring to subject them to a foreign Legislature in all Cases: but We had endangered the Liberty of France upon the Seas. Her Commerce, her Navy, her West India Islands, her Fisheries, her East India Possessions, had all been entirely at our Mercy, if North America had continued to this day a Part of the British Empire. We equally endangered the Liberty of Spain. Her Fleets, her Islands, and the Communication between her Country and her Colonies would have been in our Power. What would have become of Holland? With what unbounded contempt have we treated her? Her Liberty upon the Seas is so little respected by Us that We annull at Pleasure all Treaties ancient and modern, and seize ships without a Colour of Law. The other maritime Powers are all now more attentive to Commerce than ever. They see America is necessary to their Views of Commerce. Each one of them sees that she must have a share of American Commerce or she cannot maintain her maritime

Independency, her Liberty upon the Seas. She sees also that if any one commercial nation of Europe was to enjoy an exclusive monopoly in America, that no other maritime Power could preserve her Liberty. No wonder then that We see such Unanimity of Sentiment among the maritime Powers. No wonder that all the Sons of Neptune, are united to preserve the Independence, the Freedom and Sovereignty of his Reign from our Invasions.

5. The Growing State of the Colonies, on the Continent which appears by the Exports. The Value of the Exports from England to North America was

	£	S	d
in 1763	1,867,285	6	2
in 1771	4,586,882	17	11
Increase in eight years	2,719,597	11	9

The Value of the Exports from England to the West Indies was

	£	S	d
in 1763	1,149,596	12	4
in 1771	1,155,658	3	11
Increase in eight years	6,061	11	7

The Value of the Imports into England from the West Indies, was

	£	S	d
in 1763	3,268,485	14	6
in 1771	2,800,583	14	0
Decrease in 8 years	467,902	0	6

He could not obtain an Account of the general Exports from the West Indies, and therefore, cannot make a Comparison, with those from North America, which were

	£	S	d
in 1766	3,924,606	0	0
in 1773	6,400,000	0	0
Increase in 7 years	2,475,394	0	0

The Exports from Great Britain to foreign Countries have been generally computed at £7,000,000

	£	S	d			
in 1771 from England to America	4,586,882	15	5	£ 7,000,000		
to the W. Indies	1,155,658	9	11	5,742,530	19	4
				12,742,530	19	4

The Exports from Scotland to America are not included; when added they well increase the value of the Exports of Great Britain to Upwards of £6,000,000 which is nearly equal to the amount of all foreign Exports of the Kingdom, and one half of the whole Commerce of the nation, exclusive only of that to Ireland and the East Indies.

It is reported that the Facts and Estimates were all laid before the American Congress in the Year 1774 when the Writer was a Member. They were minutely examined and thoroughly weighed and with the most unfeigned sincerity it was wished and prayed by all, and with the most sanguine Confidence expected by many, that they would occur to our Parliament, and prevent them from disaffecting by a perseverance in Impolicy and Injustice, so precious a Part of the dominions. Others who had studied more attentively the Character of this nation, and the Relations of America with Europe, had strong Fears that nothing would succeed. They have been found to have judged right. The Americans lament the Misfortunes of the English, but they rejoice in the Prospect of superiour Liberty, Prosperity and Glory to the new World, that now opens to view, in Consequence of our Errors. They rejoice also at the destruction of that selfish and contracted Monopoly which confined the Blessings, of that Quarter of the World to a single nation and at the liberal Extension of them to all mankind.

I shall conclude all with one Observation upon the ability and Resources of America to continue the War and finally support their Independency. By the Resolutions of Congress of the 18 of March last, they redeem their two hundred millions of Paper dollars, at the Ratio of 40 Paper for one silver, which it seems is a full allowance, which makes the whole Value of their Paper Bills abroad of the Value of five millions of silver dollars, or 1,102,500 of Sterling.

They have also resolved that the Loan Office Certificates shall be paid in Proportion to the Value of the money at the time they were issued, which is the only equitable Way, and these added to the 1,002,500 in Bills and to their debt contracted in Europe makes the

whole amount of the national debt of the United States amount to
about five millions Sterling. Thus they have conducted the whole
War, for five Years for five millions, one Million a Year. According
to the Estimates of this Writer the Exports from North America in
1773 were 6,400,000 Pounds. The whole Expence of five Years War,
has not then amount to the Value of one Years export.

Compare this with our Expenses. Lord Norths Loan only this
year is Twelve Millions. According to the Estimate of this Writer
the whole Exports of Great Britain to foreign Countries North
America and the West Indies, amounted in 1771 to 12,742,530 19 4.
Thus we borrow annually to maintain the War a sum equal nearly
to our whole Exports.

Let a cool man judge, whether We or they can support the War
longest. Let us soberly reflect, what Burden this debt is to America.
It has been said that all the Colonies together, contracted in the
Course of the last French War a debt of Ten Millions, double their
present, which was all nearly discharged before this War began. Be
this as it may, I am well informed that the Province of the Massachusetts Bay alone, raised by Taxes half a Million and by Loan half
a Million more, in the Course of the last War, and before this War
broke out, it was all paid off. The Province of Massachusetts now
has double the Number of Inhabitants she had in the middle of the
last War. Let the War continue as long as it will, our debt will
accumulate twice as fast, four times as fast in Proportion to our
Abilities, as the American will. And at the End this affecting difference. That in a very few Years she will pay the utmost Farthing of
the Principal, and We shall be very happy, if We can pay the annual
Interest.

We knew not the Resources of America. We knew not the Resources in their Minds and Hearts. There are deep and great Virtues
and Profound Abilities in that People that we have not yet put to
Tryal nor called forth to Action. Her Agriculture, Manufactures and
Commerce, are Resources, that we have no Idea of. But she is now
recurring to another Resource that We neither understand nor can
bear to practice. Economy. They are striking off, every useless officer
and office in their Army their Navy, their civil departments and
otherwise to save Expenses, and in future they will conduct the War
at half the Expence of the past. America is the best Friend we can
have upon Earth. And We shall find her, if We will not suffer her
to be our Friend, our most fatal Enemy.

Letter XII

Before we dismiss these cool Thoughts, it may not be amiss to subjoin a few Reflections, upon the Certainty of American Independence.

We have repeated the Word Rebellion, untill the People have been wrought up to a Pitch of Passion and Enthusiasm, which has rendered them incapable of listening to the still Voice of Reason. Men are governed by Words. Their Passions are inflamed by Words. Policy associates certain Passions with certain Words for its own purposes. There are Words which command the Respect of Nations. Other irresistably allure their Esteem; others excite their Envy or Jealousy: and there are others that summon up all their Hatred, Contempt, Malice, and Rancour. It is only necessary to let loose a single Word to stir up Armies, Navies and nations to unlimited Rage.

The Word Rebellion has been too often repeated from the Throne, and echoed from both Houses of Parliament: too often repeated in the Prayers of the Church; in News Papers and Pamphlets, in private Conversation, and in the dispatches of our Generals and Admiralty, not to have had its full Effect. It has wrought this nation out of "its old good nature, and its old good Humour" to borrow Expressions of Lord Claredon, into a Degree of Inhumanity, that cool Posterity will condemn to Shame, and our Armies and Navies to a Series of Cruelties, which will form an indellible Blott in our History.

The Americans were fully aware, before this War broke out, of all the Consequences of the Cry of Rebellion. Our Governors and other Crown Officers took Care to instruct them in Nature and the Punishment of Treason, by elaborate Descriptions and Deffinitions in the Newspapers. There was not a circumstance in the Punishment of Treason but what was laid before the Eyes of the People at large. But all this did not succeed. Their Love of Liberty was stronger than death. They did not want to be informed in the last speech from the throne: that the Authors of all rebellious Resistance, to repeal or reform the Laws, must terminate in their Destruction or in the overthrow of the Constitution. This very cry with which we have animated ourselves and our Forces to pursue the War will operate as an eternal Barrier to any Reconciliation short of Independence. The People knew, that however plausible and specious, our Pretensions may be, if they ever submit to the Kings Government again, if it were but for an Hour, they shall be construed into Rebells and Traitors, Characters that they more universally and justly disdain, than the People of any one of the three Kingdoms.

In the civil Wars that have happened in these Kingdoms, in that for Example, which prevailed from 1641 to 1660, it originated in a Controversy between different Branches of our Legislature, and each having been an undoubted Part of our Constitution, the Nation was nearly equally divided. The Clergy were divided tho the greater Part took side with the Court. The Lawyers were equally divided. And this has ever been the position of this nation nearly ballanced between the Court and Country Party leaning sometimes to one and sometimes to the other, as the Constitution seemed to require.

But in America the Case was different. In all the Colonies the monarchical Part of their Constitutions, the Royal Governors, were generally little esteemed or confided in, by the Body of the People. The aristocratical Part, in their Councils, in those Colonies where they were elected by the Representatives, were esteemed only in Proportion as they confirmed to the Sentiments of the Representatives, in those where they were appointed by the Crown they were not esteemed at all, except by the few who flattered them in order to get offices, and these in that Country, where Men and Estates were so divided, were an inconsiderable Number. The predominant Spirit then of every Colony has been from the Beginning democratical, and the Party that ever could be obtained to decide in favour of Councils, Governors, the Royal authority or that of Parliament has ever been inconsiderable. The people ever stood by their Representatives, and what is more remarkable, the Lawyers and Clergy have almost universally taken the same side. This has been the popular Torrent, that like a River changing its bed, has irresistably born away every Thing before it. The Sentiments of this People therefore are not to be changed.

Britain changefull as a Child at Play.

Now called in Princes and then drove away, because the nation was so divided that a little good or bad success, a little Prosperity or Distress, was sufficient by changing the Sentiments or Professions of a small Number to altar the Ballance.

But if in that Case any foreign Power had intervened, if France had taken the Side of the Patriotic Party against the Royal Family, or that of the Court against he Counry and sent over to the Island sixty thousand Men and fifty sail of Men of War to its assistance what would have been the Consequence? It is most certain, that it would have decided the controversy at once.

In the Case of America, the popular Party, have a Majority in every Colony so decided, that all offices and Authority under the King, when the Period of the Revolution came to a Crisis, were hurried away before it like Leaves and Straws before the Hurricane. We have sent over more than sixty thousand Men, and a great naval Force to assist the small Party of Royalists humbled in the Dust in order to make a Ballance. Were they able to succeed? Did they ever produce the least Simpton of Doubt or Hesitation in the Body of the People of the final success of their Cause. But now by the Inter- position of France and Spain, our Forces by Sea and Land, are so employed, our Resources so exhausted, We have called off so much of our Force for the defence of the West India Islands, that our whole Force is inconsiderable. The French themselves have a Sea Force there perhaps equal to ours, and a Land Force, which amounts to a great deal. What have We then to expect? It is obvious to all Europe that France and Spain, or either of them have it in their Power to finish all our Hopes in North America, whenever they please, and compleat the Triumph of the Patriotic Party there. And they have motives so urgent to do it, that We may depend upon it they will. Why then are we putting ourselves to an infinite Expence to keep New York and Charlestown? If we wait for the People to declare in our favour, we shall wait like the Jews, for a Messiah that will never come, or like the Countryman who waited for the last drops of the River.

When we see that even the Inhabitants of New York are distrusted by our Generals; when they dare not confide to them Ammunition and Arms. When we see that all our Arts and all our Terrors, added to all the Joys of our Partizans, and all the sorrows of the Patriots, could obtain only 210 Names to an Address out of 120 thousand Inhabitants in Carolina. And when Clinton himself tells Us that Parties were lingering in the Province, and Magistrates under the late Government endeavouring to execute the Laws? Do you suppose the great states of N. Carolina, Virginia and Maryland will be idle?

Will not the Congress exert themselves to relieve Carolina and Georgia at the very Time, when the Spaniards are marching with slow but sure steps through the Floridas, and New York will be blocked up with a French Fleet. The combined naval armaments of Spain and France may be an overmatch for Rodney. Gibraltar is suffering in heroic Patience and D'Estaing putting the channel Fleet and this Island in Danger.

Appendix:

The Affair of the Anonymous Letter

Circulating derogatory anonymous information, as Henry Laurens accused Edmund Jenings of doing, is a familiar tactic of intelligence services and of partisans eager to demoralize their opponents. During the American Revolution a stream of anonymous, poison pen letters were directed at the diplomatic representatives of the United States. "There has been an uninterrupted succession of them," John Adams wrote Laurens on August 15, 1782, "ever since I have been in Europe." [1] Among the Adams Papers alone, in the space of seven months, between November 1781 and May 1782, there are five inflammatory anonymous letters. What is remarkable about these letters, with three of which Jenings is linked, either by his admission or by accusations of others, is their effectiveness. They exacerbated differences between Adams and Franklin and between Adams and the French, and one of them irritated a wound which, after long festering, broke open into an estrangement between Adams and Laurens. To examine these anonymous letters, to consider why and how they worked their mischief, is to add an informative footnote to the diplomacy of the American Revolution.

The impact of the anonymous letters on Adams is graphically demonstrated by his reaction to an epistle which Jenings sent him on November 14, 1781, written, allegedly, by "a Person of some Distinction at Paris to a Man not less so in London." [2] The identity of the principals Jenings professed not to know. Adams flattered

---

[1] John Adams, *The Works of John Adams, Second President of the United States*, ed. Charles Francis Adams, 10 vols. (Freeport, N.Y.: Books for Libraries Press, 1969), 7:611.
[2] Jenings to Adams, November 14, 1781, Adams Papers microfilm, reel 355.

himself that they were the comte de Vergennes and Lord Shelburne.[3]
The letter attacked Adams:

"Nous de donnons pas à Monsieur Ad[ams] une Confiance bien aveugle; et ce
n'est pas sans cause qu'ils ont mis autour de lui des Hommes, qui l'observent;
on le croit honnête; on le scait ardent, inflexible même pour sa Cause; mais il
il s'abonde trop dans son sens, et ne scait donner aux convenances. Nous aimons
mieux placer Confiance dans Monsieur Fra[nklin]."

Adams never doubted that the letter was genuine, for it con-
formed to his own perception of French attitudes toward Franklin
and himself. By the fall of 1781 he was convinced that France
wanted to reduce the United States to a demeaning dependency
upon her and that Vergennes and his colleagues were attempting
to undermine him because he refused to acquiesce in their designs.
Franklin, Adams believed, was a French tool whose malleability
accounted for his enormous and, to him, intolerable popularity in
France. The writer of the anonymous letter was obviously someone close enough to Adams to know his jaundiced attitude toward
Franklin and the French. Playing to it in the letter of November
14 made it credible to Adams while at the same time it corrobo-
rated his views of French hostility toward him and increased his
distaste for Vergennes and Franklin, which (the letter writer must
have hoped) would obstruct his cooperation with both and retard
the progress of allied diplomacy.

The November 14 letter etched itself in Adams's mind. He quoted
from it in a letter to Secretary of Foreign Affairs Livingston on
February 21, 1782,[4] and used phrases from it in his correspondence
at intervals thereafter.[5] In a letter to Elbridge Gerry of May 2, 1785,
Adams repeated the entire letter from memory.[6] By this time he
had decided that, by stressing his uncompromising independence,
the letter was a high compliment and not a criticism, as its author
had intended.

The letter of November 14, 1781, sharpened the edge of an animosity which already existed. That of May 3, 1782, mentioned
above in the essay introducing the Distinguished American letters,
was considerably more of a catalyst in the creation of hostility between Adams and one of his colleagues. The May 3 letter attacked
Adams:

---

[3] *Boston Patriot*, November 17, 1810.

[4] John Adams, *Works*, 7:525.

[5] To Jenings, September 27, 1782; April 18, 1783, Adams Papers microfilm,
reels 358, 108.

[6] To Gerry, May 2, 1785, ibid., reel 364.

"Sir,
You have a friend who has suffered too much from the particular situation he
was in lately, not to interest every honest man in his behalf to prevent his being
the dupe of artifice. He has already been ill treated from a quarter unlooked for
and the same game is continued to answer the end first proposed. American ministers in Europe have various politicks to pursue and some of them understand
best those that can serve their interest. Adams envious of every superior merit
has much labour'd clandestinely in injuring Franklin and Laurens to secure his
situation and answer further ends. And by the means he has used has perhaps
succeeded better than in serving the interest of his Country here, where his business has been done by others, for however great his abilities as a lawyer they are
the reverse as a Minister. Be discreet in giving Mr. Laurens a caution from that
quarter, and at another time you shall be apprised of the secret of a conduct
which is every way base and dishonourable." [7]

This letter surfaced on May 17, 1782, when Edward Bridgen, a
London merchant, received it "by the Foreign Mail . . . in a dis-
guished hand." [8] The writer of the letter intended Bridgen to com-
municate its contents to his friend "who has suffered too much
from the particular situation he was in lately." This was Henry
Laurens, who had only recently been released from the Tower of
London. The letter writer must, then, have been one of small company who knew that Bridgen was a conduit to Laurens. Jenings
was an "intimate acquaintance" of Bridgen who had used him to
convey messages from Adams to Laurens.[9] Therefore, Bridgen assumed, upon receiving the letter, that it had been sent, though not
necessarily written, by Jenings.[10]

Bridgen sent the letter to Laurens, who had left London on May
11, 1782, for the Netherlands,[11] where he intended to do what he
could to execute the minister plenipotentiary's powers with which
Congress had vested him in 1779 and which his capture at sea by the
British on his way to Europe in 1780 had prevented him from dis-
charging. The letter overtook Laurens in Antwerp, where he stop-
ped for a few days to recover from a brief illness.[12] "I can easily tell,"

---

[7] Enclosed with Jenings to Adams, June 6, 1782, ibid., reel 357.

[8] Henry Laurens, *Mr. Laurens's True State of the Case. By Which His Candor
to Mr. Edmund Jenings is Manifested, and the Tricks of Mr. Jenings Are Detected* (London, 1783), pp. 7–8, Rare Book and Special Collections Division,
Library of Congress. Hereafter cited as Laurens pamphlet.

[9] Laurens pamphlet, p. 35. For the Jenings-Bridgen-Laurens connection, see
Bridgen to Adams, July 13, 1781; Jenings to Adams, November 28, December 24,
1781; Adams to Jenings, February 21, 1782, Adams Papers microfilm, reels 355,
356.

[10] Laurens pamphlet, pp. 22, 61.

[11] Laurens to Benjamin Franklin, June 24, 1782, U.S. Department of State,
The Revolutionary Diplomatic Correspondence of the United States, ed. Francis
Wharton, 6 vols. (Washington: Government Printing Office, 1889), 5:504.

[12] Laurens gave conflicting accounts about when he received the letter. At one

he told a companion, "who sent it to Mr. Bridgen; by his description, it must be his friend Jenings." [13] It is not clear whether Laurens initially believed that Jenings had written the letter or had merely transmitted it.

Laurens conferred with Adams in The Hague during the first days of June. Despite his protests that the meeting had gone well, that Adams had received him with the "utmost cordiality," and that "we parted as we had met . . . in perfect friendship," [14] the meeting left a bad taste in Laurens's mouth. Adams's conduct appears, in fact, to have been indefensible. Appointed minister to the Dutch when Congress learned of Laurens's capture, Adams had managed to obtain diplomatic recognition in April 1782. He had also received from Congress on June 20, 1780, a provisional commission to borrow money in the Netherlands, to be effective "until the said Henry Laurens, or some other person appointed in his stead, shall arrive in Europe and undertake the execution of the said commission. . . ." [15] When Laurens arrived in Holland, Adams was in the last stage of concluding an agreement with three Dutch banking houses for a loan. Rather than let Laurens participate and share the credit for borrowing the desperately needed money, Adams refused to show him his commission (Laurens had thrown his copies overboard when the British captured him), contenting himself with briefing Laurens about how things were going. Having nothing to do, Laurens left Adams and went to Brussels, where he arrived on June 7 and stayed for a week. [16]

According to Jenings, who was then living at Brussels and seems to have spent much of the week of June 7 with Laurens, Laurens was "manifestly" unhappy—close to rage, in fact [17]—that Adams

---

place in his pamphlet he declared that "on the 1st of June last, at Antwerp, I received from a friend in London, a copy of an anonymous letter (p. 30)." At another he said that he became ill at Antwerp "on the night of the 22d May," that he was detained there for a day or two, and that during that period he received the letter (pp. 6, 10).

[13] Laurens pamphlet, pp. 7–8.

[14] Ibid., p. 8.

[15] U.S. Department of State, *The Revolutionary Diplomatic Correspondence*, 4:61.

[16] Jenings to Adams, June 20, 1782, Adams Papers microfilm, reel 357.

[17] Edmund Jenings, *The Candor of Henry Laurens, Esq; Manifested by his Behaviour to Mr. Edmund Jenings* (London, 1783), pp. 15–16, Rare Book and Special Collections Division, Library of Congress; hereafter cited as Jenings pamphlet I; Edmund Jenings, *A Full Manifestation of What Mr. Henry Laurens Falsely Denominates Candor in Himself, and Tricks in Mr. Edmund Jenings* (London, 1783), pp. 37, 47, 52, Rare Book and Special Collections Division, Library of Congress; hereafter cited as Jenings pamphlet II.

had not shown him the commissions for the Dutch mission. Having had the commissions himself and having assisted in drafting them while in Congress, he knew that he was named in them and given authority to act by them. He complained about Adams's secrecy to Jenings [18] and to Franklin as well, who wondered "a little at Mr. [Adams] not acquainting you whether your name was in the commission or not." [19] Laurens's resentment of Adams percolated just beneath his protestations of regard for him, breaking out in occasional jabs like that to Jenings of August 11, 1782, that he had "waited upom Him [Adams] at a great expence and made a tender of my Services" and would have taken the Dutch mission had it been offered; still, "what happened was by no means a disappointment to myself," he assured Jenings, even though he was puzzled that Adams had not written him a "single Line" about the Dutch mission since 1779, although many occasions "have offered." [20]

When Jenings was with Laurens at Brussels, he questioned him so aggressively about his interviews with Adams that he aroused his suspicions.[21] His first question was, had Laurens seen the anonymous letter of May 3, 1782 (Bridgen had sent a copy of the letter to Jenings, who received it by May 23 and sent it on to Adams)? [22] Then he asked Laurens "Why I had not remained in Holland, and engaged in the prosecution of the Loan for the United States? and Whether Mr. Adams had shewn me his Commission?" [23] Laurens was "much disturbed by these interrogatories," which he regarded as "extremely improper." [24] It appeared, in fact, to Laurens that Jenings was trying "to make an impression upon my mind unfavourable to Mr. Adams" and that he was "much disappointed" when he failed.[25] Jenings's eager questions about the anonymous letter persuaded Laurens not only that had he transmitted it to Bridgen but also that he had written it himself. "I perceived in the first instant," Laurens wrote to Adams on August 25, 1782, that "he [Bridgen] had

---

[18] Jenings pamphlet II, 54; Jenings to Adams, August 29, 1782, Adams Papers microfilm, reel 357.
[19] Laurens to Franklin, June 24, 1782; Franklin to Laurens, July 2, 1782, U.S. Department of State, *Revolutionary Diplomatic Correspondence*, 5: 503, 590; for Adams's defense of his actions, see his letter to Jenings, August 30, 1782, Adams Papers microfilm, reel 357.
[20] To Jenings, August 11, 1782, ibid.
[21] Laurens pamphlet, pp. 9, 56.
[22] Jenings pamphlet II, p. 19.
[23] Laurens pamphlet, p. 9.
[24] Ibid., pp. 9, 56.
[25] Ibid., p. 10.

been bubbled, and with the mind's eye as instantly fixed upon the man who had attempted to bamboozle, perhaps to embroil us all. . . ." [26] That man, Laurens was certain, was Edmund Jenings.

Laurens left Brussels on June 14 for the south of France, assuming that he had put the anonymous letter behind him. He had, he told Jenings in Brussels, "been with Mr. Adams nearly a week, and had not mentioned it to him, and determined never to mention it; it was the work of a vile incendiary, and should be treated with contempt." [27] But it would not be as easy as Laurens thought to sink the letter "in oblivion as the most effectual means of disappointing the malevolent designs of the authors." [28]

Adams, having received a copy of the letter from Jenings, mulled it over and, evidently feeling guilty about his treatment of Laurens, requested Jenings on July 20, 1782, to write him and tell him "that all that is said by the anonimous scribbler is a Lye. That if he will accept of this Mission I will resign it in a Moment. That I love and esteem him, and ever did, and have ever publickly and privately avowed it." [29] Jenings duly discharged this request and another of August 30, 1782, in which Adams asked him to inform Laurens about the specifics of his Dutch commissions. Laurens resented Jenings's letters, implying that Adams had not really designated him as an intermediary [30] and declaring that he was "intermeddling" where he had no business, that his efforts amounted to "impertinent officiousness." [31] He believed that Jenings was either trying to keep the poison of the anonymous letters potent or, by interceding between Adams and him, attempting to get credit for healing "a breach . . . which had never existed." [32] The anonymous letter refused to go away. The subject "has rather wound me up," Laurens wrote Jenings on August 5, 1782,[33] and he now resolved to investigate it further when he returned to London, where he would see Bridgen, the original recipient of the letter.

Meeting Bridgen in London in September, Laurens interrogated him about the letter. "Will Lee of Bruxelles" wrote it, Bridgen vol-

---

[26] Laurens to Adams, August 25, 1782, Adams Papers microfilm, reel 357; Laurens pamphlet, p. 33.
[27] Ibid., p. 10.
[28] Ibid., p. 9.
[29] Adams to Jenings, July 20, 1782, Adams Papers microfilm, reel 357.
[30] Laurens pamphlet, p. 12.
[31] Ibid., pp. 10, 18–19.
[32] Ibid., pp. 27, 57.
[33] Ibid., p. 15.

unteered.[34] How did he know that, Laurens asked? Jenings had implied as much in a letter, Bridgen answered. Laurens refused to believe that Lee was the author of the anonymous letter. Rather, he concluded that Jenings, Lee's accuser, was the author, reasoning that if Jenings, who lived with his cousin William Lee, in Brussels "upon the most friendly terms," was capable of "slandering him to Mr. Bridgen, accusing him of writing the anonymous letter, and calling him a villain," he was equally capable of maligning his friend Adams.[35] Bridgen was later compelled to admit that he was on shaky grounds in ascribing the accusation against William Lee to Jenings. "It did not appear," he conceded, "that Mr. Jenings . . . had actually accused Mr. Lee of writing the anonymous letter, or called him a villain." Nevertheless, Bridgen insisted that Jenings had insinuated as much.[36] Laurens's position was one of not wanting to be confused by the facts, for he refused to read any of Jenings's letters to Bridgen in which the insinuation against Lee were said to have been contained. Jenings consistently and resolutely denied that he had ever accused Lee of anything.[37]

Fortified in his convictions of Jenings's guilt, Laurens resolved to expose him when he returned to Paris in the latter part of November to participate in the peace negotiations with the British. Making a midnight appearance at the negotiations, Laurens arrived in Paris on November 29, 1782. After the preliminaries were signed the next day, he called on Adams and related his suspicions of Jenings. Adams immediately visited Jenings to relay Laurens's charges.[38] Adams refused to believe them and never wavered in his conviction of Jenings's innocence.[39] Laurens was piqued by Adams's refusal to credit him—"this is all very pretty drama," he sarcastically remarked—and "a day or two" later he went to Franklin, to whom he "related the affair of the anonymous letter with all its concomitant circumstances . . . as well as to impart to him my suspicions of Mr. Jenings, as to take his opinion and advice upon the subject."[40] The doctor produced an anonymous letter of his own, from one WR,

---

[34] Ibid., p. 20.

[35] Ibid., p. 27.

[36] Ibid., p. 27n.

[37] Jenings pamphlet II, p. 35.

[38] Jenings pamphlet I, p. 6; Laurens pamphlet, p. 36. It should be noted that, in his pamphlet, Laurens dates the interview with Adams December 8, 1782. Ibid., p. 27.

[39] Jenings pamphlet I, p. 6.

[40] Laurens pamphlet, p. 40.

dated at Amsterdam, January 31, 1782, but postmarked at Brussels, Jenings's domicile. It scored Adams for abusing Franklin and for botching his embassy in the Netherlands. Its purpose, evidently, was the same as that of the anonymous letter of May 3, 1782: to create dissention between the American ministers.

Upon examining the letter of January 31, 1782, Laurens concluded that Jenings had written it, because several changes in it were "so very like Mr. Jenings's corrections, which I had seen in above twenty instances in his letters to me, that I could not hesitate a moment to say, I was as sure the performance was his as I could be sure of his handwriting." [41] Jenings denied that he had written this letter, but Laurens, persuaded by the handwriting that he had, was strengthened in his belief that he had also written the letter of May 3, 1782.

Laurens now decided that he had sufficient proof against Jenings to give William Lee a chance to repudiate the charge that he had written the letter of May 3. Accordingly, Laurens wrote Lee on December 21, 1782. Replying on December 24, Lee indignantly denied that he had written the letter and demanded the name of his accuser. On December 28 Laurens answered that Lee must apply to Bridgen for it. On the same day Adams called on Laurens to discuss Lee. Adams absolved him of guilt. The conversation turned to Jenings, whose innocence Adams persisted in declaring, finally affirming "I cannot believe that person is guilty; but the thing is in a way now, and must go on." [42]

Apparently at Adams's urging, Jenings called on Laurens the next day. Laurens explicitly accused him of writing the letter of May 3; just as explicitly Jenings denied his charges.[43] A considerable correspondence between the two men ensued, the result of which was that they agreed to lay their differences before mutual friends, who would mediate the dispute. Consequently, on January 6, 1783, Jenings, with Matthew Ridley as his representative, met Laurens who enlisted the services of Richard Oswald, an old business associate and, most recently, British peace negotiator. (None of the conferees apparently found it odd that a British diplomat should adjudicate claims that the confidant of one of his opposite numbers had attempted to create dissension in the American negotiating team that

---

[41] Ibid., pp. 28–29.
[42] Ibid., p. 36.
[43] Jenings pamphlet I, p. 9 ff.

would redound to Britain's benefit.) After a brief discussion Laurens and Jenings decided to see if they could compose the quarrel by themselves. They retired to a private room and after Laurens enumerated his reasons for suspecting Jenings, the question arose of whether Jenings transmitted the letter of May 3 to Adams on his own initiative. He swore that he had not, that he had transmitted it at Bridgen's *"particular desire."* " 'If that be the case,' " replied Laurens, who claimed that he now wanted "to get rid of" Jenings, " 'the face of affairs is greatly changed. . . . Bridgen . . . has committed himself horribly . . . ; but this being the case, Sir, I am satisfied with respect to you.' " [44] Having been exonerated (he thought), Jenings shook Laurens's hand and hugged Oswald, who was waiting in an adjoining room. Good cheer reigned. But the books were far from closed on the anonymous letter of May 3, 1782.

In January 1783 Jenings went to Brussels to confront William Lee, who evidently had been told by Bridgen that Jenings had accused him of writing the anonymous letter. Jenings apparently expected to be challenged to a duel, for he later wrote that he had been "obliged to come to Brussels to defend my life" and reproached Bridgen for almost causing the "shedding of relations blood." [45] Jenings reported to Adams from Brussels, January 23, 1783, that Lee was treating him with studied coolness,[46] but violence was apparently avoided, for Jenings was in London by February 21, 1783,[47] where he resided until his death in 1819.

Laurens preceded Jenings to London, arriving there on January 16, 1783.[48] He sought out Bridgen and asked him: "How came you my good friend to desire Mr. Jenings to send that cursed anonymous letter to Mr. Adams which has occasioned so much trouble?" [49] Bridgen emphatically denied that Jenings had transmitted the letter to Adams at his request as Jenings had told Laurens at the interview in Paris. When Jenings arrived in London, Bridgen challenged his version of the transmission of the letter. Jenings admitted that he had told Laurens that he had acted at Bridgen's request and that Bridgen had, in fact, made no such request: "He thought he might

---

[44] For a full account of the interview of January 6, 1783, see Laurens pamphlet, pp. 60–63.

[45] Jenings pamphlet I, pp. 7, 25; pamphlet II, pp. 9, 28.

[46] To Adams, January 23, 1783, Adams Papers microfilm, reel 360.

[47] To Adams, March 14, 1783, ibid.

[48] Laurens to Jenings, January 24, 1783, ibid.

[49] Ibid.

take such a liberty with him," he told Bridgen.[50] This confession confirmed Laurens's worst suspicions of Jenings. On March 6, 1783, he wrote Adams, laying out the new evidence that Jenings was a lying scoundrel and renewing his charge that he wrote the anonymous letter of May 3, 1782. Laurens's aim, he admonished Adams, was not "to blast Mr. Jenings's Character but to undeceive you & to prevent, if possible, the progress of further evils, from his influence over or interference in our Councils & deliberations." The anonymous letter, Laurens continued in a tone which must have made Adams wince, was "contrived not merely for the purpose of slandering Mr. Adams. The grand view was to excite jealousy and by degrees to produce animosity among us all, Mr. Adams in the mean time to be played upon & hoodwinked by an excess of flattery. How far in my apprehension the scheme succeeded I shall candidly intimate, if you desire it, the next time I have the honor of conversing with you." [51]

Adams, in effect, dismissed Laurens's charges. Replying to him on March 12, 1783, he waived them off with the remark that "it is a Mystery which Time will unriddle and to Time I leave it. . . ." [52] Adams's cavalier attitude angered Laurens and produced a sharp letter of March 26, 1783, enclosing a certificate from Bridgen attesting that Jenings had admitted lying about the transmission of the May 3, 1782, letter. "You will hereafter receive a copy of a Letter from Mr. Bridgen in confirmation of what I said to you in my last," wrote Laurens. "If after this there shall still remain in your opinion a 'Mystery which Time only can unriddle,' it must so rest with you." Laurens told Adams, "Time has acted his part. If We affect to disbelieve the Evidence which he has brought forth, neither will we be persuaded tho' one rose from the dead." [53] He construed Adams's refusal to credit his charges as an insulting reflection on his judgment. His anger with Adams over the ascription of the identity of the anonymous letter writer was precisely the mischief which he believed the libeller had intended to produce: the setting of one American commissioner against another.

Jenings, who had been reporting to Adams from London on British politics, soon learned of Laurens's "fresh Attack . . . on my

---

[50] Laurens to Adams, March 6, 1783, ibid.
[51] Ibid.
[52] Adams to Laurens, March 12, 1783, ibid., reel 108.
[53] Laurens to Adams, March 26, 1783, ibid., reel 360.

reputation." [54] To justify himself, he decided to write a pamphlet, informing Adams on June 3 that he was "drawing up a simple Narrative of this whole Transaction with necessary quotations." [55] In deciding to go public, Jenings did not serve his best interests. On December 28, 1782, Laurens declared that only six people (himself, Jenings, Bridgen, Adams, Lee, and Franklin) knew of the controversy; by March 1783 knowledge of it was still confined to the same small circle.[56] It would have been to Jenings's advantage had the facts remained this closely held. Although his defense was spirited— he affirmed that his erroneous claim that he had sent the anonymous letter to Adams at Bridgen's instigation was an innocent mistake and not a willful falsehood and scored several points against Laurens— he laid himself open to a public rejoinder by Laurens in which his alleged transgressions were broadcast across Europe and America by a man whose reputation was far greater than his own. In what was essentially a contest of one man's word against another's, Laurens, a former president of the Continental Congress whose capture and confinement in the Tower of London had made him an international celebrity and martyr of the American cause, Laurens, the hero, would overbear an obscure man like Jenings.

Jenings's pamphlet, *The Candor of Henry Laurens, Esq; Manifested by his Behaviour to Mr. Edmund Jenings*, was published by July 7, 1783.[57] Laurens replied at considerably greater length in a work entitled *Mr. Laurens's True State of the Case. By Which His Candor to Mr. Edmund Jenings Is Manifested, and the Tricks of Mr. Jenings Are Detected.* Dated September 3, 1783, Laurens's pamphlet showered Jenings with the severest accusations: he was an unprincipled office seeker—he "aimed at an important public employment, in which he might have collected secrets of state, the thirst of his soul, for private purposes;" [58] he "practiced the most cunning devices for exciting jealousies between the American Ministers;" [59] he was "unworthy of public confidence, and . . . a dan-

---

54 Jenings to Adams, June 3, 1783, ibid., reel 361.

55 Ibid.

56 Laurens pamphlet, p. 34; Laurens to Adams, March 6, 1783, Adams Papers, microfilm, reel 360.

57 So Jenings wrote Adams. The edition in the Rare Book and Special Collection Division, Library of Congress, contains introductory and closing notes by Jenings, dated July 29, 1783, which suggest a typographical error or a second edition. Jenings to Adams, July 7, 22, 1783, ibid., reel 361.

58 Laurens pamphlet, p. 4.

59 Ibid., pp. 4, 5.

gerous confidant to a Minister of State;" [60] he was, gravest charge of all, "a traitor." [61] Laurens's pamphlet reflected almost as unfavorably on Adams as it did upon Jenings, for it dilated on Jenings's "influence over Mr. Adams" [62] and described Laurens as being "desirous of delivering Mr. Adams from the fascination under which he had been too long held by that false friend, and as I feared, to the detriment of our country. . . ." [63] In a letter to Secretary of Foreign Affairs Robert Livingston of September 11, 1783, warning against Jenings, so that he might be prevented "from obtaining any Commission in the service of the United States," Laurens continued to criticize Adams. "A sense of Duty to my Country and a sincere regard for Mr. Adams," he wrote, "led me to attempt to open his Eyes. . . . I do not esteem it a trifling affair to remove a wicked mischievious favorite from his influence in our Councils," [64] to which charge Jenings correctly observed that it had as "its object the creating of jealousy and distrust, in the breast of Congress, of one of their actual Ministers." [65]

To Laurens's pamphlet Jenings wrote a detailed and often tedious refutation, *A Full Manifestation of What Mr. Henry Laurens Falsely Denominates Candor in Himself, and Tricks in Mr. Edmund Jenings*, which was published sometime before the end of 1783. In this rebuttal, Jenings called attention to two more anonymous letters which Adams had received in 1782, one dated at Ghent, May 8, 1782, the other at Paris, May 20, 1782. [66] These letters did not accuse Adams of abusing his colleagues; rather they were personal attacks, blasting him for incompetence and even for mental debility. Jenings claimed that these two letters had been compared at Paris with the anonymous one to Franklin of January 31, 1782, which Laurens accused him of writing, "by five American Gentlemen of, at least, equal credit, discernment and judgement, and more impartiality than he [Laurens] has in the question," who concluded that none of the three were in his handwriting and that "the matter of them, shews they came from Amsterdam, and, that on comparing them

[60] Ibid., p. 59.
[61] Ibid., p. 59.
[62] Ibid., p. 27.
[63] Ibid., p. 67.
[64] Laurens to Livingston, September 11, 1783, Papers of the Continental Congress microfilm, reel 117, National Archives and Records Service.
[65] Jenings pamphlet II, p. 76.
[66] Adams Papers microfilm, reel 357.

with several letters written by a man in that city, two of the gentlemen strongly suspect, and three of them verily believe, he is the
author." [67] Establishing that the January 31, 1782, letter was not
written by Jenings removed, of course, a major prop for Laurens's
contention that he was the author of the May 3, 1782, letter, since
Laurens argued that the authorship of the former proved the latter.

Franklin supplied additional information about the handwriting
comparison session. He stated that he believed that it occurred at
Auteuil, in suburban Paris, where Adams was recovering from an
illness in September and October 1783 as the house guest of American consul general to France Thomas Barclay.[68] According to
Franklin, Matthew Ridley called on him and asked to borrow the
letter of January 31, 1782. He returned with it some days later, convinced that it was in the handwriting of a clerk employed by the
Amsterdam merchant-banker and longtime friend of America, John
de Neufville. Franklin supposed that Adams, Barclay, and Ridley,
all friends of Jenings's, had conducted the investigation.[69] The two
other American participants named by Jenings can not be identified.
That the anonymous letters were ascribed to Amsterdam points to
Adams's role in the investigation, for he had, from the first interview
with Laurens in December 1782, assumed that they were the "work
of a set of villains in Amsterdam." [70] In April 1784 he became more
specific, pointing the finger at an "Anglo-Norman" in de Neufville's
banking house, but he named no names.[71]

Comparing handwriting, however, only convinced those already
committed to Jenings's innocence. Franklin, upon being shown what
Ridley took to be the exculpatory evidence, did not think that the
similarities between the anonymous letters and those of de Neufville's clerk were "very striking." [72] Laurens, to whom Franklin sent
the anonymous letter of January 31, 1782, and two letters from de
Neufville's clerk, thought that they did not exonerate Jenings in the
least. "An investigation is now of little moment," he exclaimed to
Franklin, "since that Man remains incontrovertibly convicted of
Crimes more heinous than would be the writing of an anonymous

67 Jenings pamphlet II, p. 79.

68 John Adams, *The Diary and Autobiography of John Adams*, ed. Lyman
Butterfield, 4 vols. (Cambridge: Harvard University Press, 1961), 3:143–46.

69 Franklin to Laurens, December 6, 1783, Franklin Papers, Miscellaneous V,
Manuscript Division, Library of Congress.

70 Laurens pamphlet, pp. 27–28.

71 Adams to ——, April 9, 1784, Adams Papers microfilm, reel 362.

72 To Laurens, December 6, 1783, Franklin Papers, Miscellaneous V.

Letter with a view of putting an injured person upon his guard against a flattering deceitful friend." "I have heard nothing concerning Jenings," Laurens continued on February 3, 1784, but "his Associate and sole Countenancer shall hear from me." [73]

And hear from Laurens Adams did, in a letter of the same day, as rough and threatening as any he ever received. Laurens was provoked by Adams's failure to forward two letters addressed to him, which he had opened, apparently inadvertently. "The first Act," he wrote, "was in every view indelicate and unjustifiable, in one, unmanly and cruel: but the long neglect, amounting to a refusal, to deliver them, is a high aggravation containing an unsufferable degree of contempt. Possibly, Sir, the patience extended on my part under this and other injurious treatment on yours, may have led you to mistake forbearance for tameness which you might play with; nor can I in any other manner reconcile your conduct with the hazard attending it." [74] Although the "hazard" with which Laurens threatened Adams did not materialize, his letter shows how far he had been "alienated" from Adams by the affair of the anonymous letters.[75]

The pamphlet battle caused relations between Jenings, on the one side, and Laurens and Bridgen, on the other, to deteriorate to the point that on May 6, 1784, Jenings challenged both to a duel.[76] What precipitated the challenge is not clear. Jenings writes mysteriously of Laurens and Bridgen seeking satisfaction from him "at the Hands of others." And he speaks of the "violence" of his adversaries, in a letter to Adams of May 7, 1784, requesting that "should the worst happen to me, I trust your Excellency will not suffer my Memory to be insulted." [77] Matters, however, did not proceed to extremities. "If the Meeting had been had," Jenings assured Adams on May 11, 1784, he would not "have injured either of my Enemies." [78]

The May 11, 1784, letter was the next to the last one which Adams received from Jenings. The final one, enclosing remarks of Arthur Lee on the foreign debt of the United States, was written on June 23, 1784, almost a full year before Adams arrived in London as Ameri-

---

[73] Laurens to Franklin, February 3, 1784, Franklin Papers, Miscellaneous VI.
[74] Laurens to Adams, February 3, 1784, Adams Papers microfilm, reel 362.
[75] Adams to ——, April 9, 1784, ibid.
[76] Jenings to Bridgen, May 6, 1784, ibid.
[77] Jenings to Adams, May 7, 1784, ibid.
[78] Jenings to Adams, May 11, 1784, ibid.

can ambassador to the Court of St. James. What caused Jenings to stop writing Adams? Laurens's assaults may have made him gun-shy about continuing to interest himself in public affairs. On January 23, 1783, for example, he told Adams of his reluctance to report to him on British politics, "being fearful after what has happened, to bring on myself fresh attacks." [79] Laurens had so blackened Jenings's reputation, moreover, that any public official who associated with him might find his own judgment and motives suspect.[80] Thus, it could be that Jenings drew away from Adams as a selfless act to protect his friend's reputation. On the other hand, if Jenings was a malevolent figure, if he was a British agent of some description, he could have used Laurens's charges as a pretext to put distance between himself and his former correspondent.

Adams, plainly, was unhappy with the cooling of his relationship with Jenings. As early as May 16, 1783, he complained that "it is a long time since I have received a Line from you" [81] and on February 10, 1784, he urged him to "tell me the News and Speculate as you used to do." [82] Adams continued to defend his friend: "I have ever vindicated your Character as far as lay in my Power," he wrote him on May 13, 1784, "from the Suspicion of having written that anonymous Libel . . . and I shall ever continue to vindicate it, because I believe you as innocent of it, as an Angel in Heaven and incapable of such a Business." [83] When Adams took up residence in London in the summer of 1785, he saw to it that Jenings was invited often to the American "embassy," where guests reported meeting him.[84] And soon after Adams returned to America in 1788, he procured Jenings's election to the American Academy of Arts and Sciences.[85]

The opinion one forms of Jenings will determine how he views Adams's extraordinary loyalty to him. If Jenings was a faithful American who tried diligently to serve his country in a time of crisis only to be maligned unfairly and relentlessly by a powerful

79 Jenings to Adams, January 23, 1783, ibid., reel 360.

80 For Jenings's awareness of this possibility, see his letter to Adams, July 22, 1783, ibid., reel 361, and Jenings pamphlet II, p. 66.

81 Adams to Jenings, May 16, 1783, Adams Papers microfilm, reel 108.

82 Adams to Jenings, February 10, 1784, ibid., reel 107.

83 Adams to Jenings, May 13, 1784, ibid.

84 Thomas Lee Shippen to [Richard Henry Lee?], August 22, 1787, Shippen Papers, Manuscript Division, Library of Congress.

85 Eliphalet Pearson to Jenings, June 15, 1789, Jenings Family Papers, 1737–1837, section 2, Virginia Historical Society, Richmond, Virginia.

man whose notions about him at times seemed to partake of paranoid delusions, Adams's steadfastness was magnificent. If Laurens, on the other hand, was right, then Adams's devotion to Jenings was stubborn folly, full of dangers to the public and to himself. Edmund Jenings humbles the historian, who must admit, at last, that he does not have the evidence to decide what kind of man he was, even as he does not have the evidence to decide who wrote the anonymous letters which so sorely taxed the American diplomats of the Revolution.

ADVISORY COMMITTEE

Library of Congress
American Revolution Bicentennial Program

John R. Alden
James B. Duke Professor of History Emeritus, Duke University

Julian P. Boyd
Editor of *The Papers of Thomas Jefferson*, Princeton University

Lyman H. Butterfield
Editor in Chief Emeritus of *The Adams Papers*, Massachusetts Historical Society

Jack P. Greene
Andrew W. Mellon Professor in the Humanities, The Johns Hopkins University

Merrill Jensen
Editor of *The Documentary History of the Ratification of the Constitution*

Cecelia M. Kenyon
Charles N. Clark Professor of Government, Smith College

Aubrey C. Land
University Research Professor, University of Georgia

Edmund S. Morgan
Sterling Professor of History, Yale University

Richard B. Morris
Gouverneur Morris Professor of History Emeritus, Columbia University

George C. Rogers, Jr.
Yates Snowden Professor of American History, University of South Carolina

☆ U.S. GOVERNMENT PRINTING OFFICE : 1978 O—258-909